# VLAKPLAAS

## APARTHEID DEATH SQUADS 1979–1994



ROBIN BINCKES

Pen & Sword
MILITARY

First published in Great Britain in 2018 by
PEN AND SWORD MILITARY
*an imprint of*
Pen and Sword Books Ltd
47 Church Street
Barnsley
South Yorkshire S70 2AS



ISBN 978 1 526729 21 7



Typeset by Aura Technology and Software Services, India
Map by Genevieve Edwards
Printed and bound by CPI Group (UK) Ltd, Croydon

Pen & Sword Books Ltd incorporates the imprints of Pen & Sword Archaeology, Atlas, Aviation, Battleground, Discovery, Family History, History, Maritime, Military, Naval, Politics, Railways, Select, Social History, Transport, True Crime, Claymore Press, Frontline Books, Leo Cooper, Praetorian Press, Remember When, Seaforth Publishing and Wharncliffe.

*For a complete list of Pen and Sword titles please contact*
Pen and Sword Books Limited
47 Church Street, Barnsley, South Yorkshire, S70 2AS, England
email: enquiries@pen-and-sword.co.uk
website: www.pen-and-sword.co.uk

# CONTENTS

SOUTHERN AFRICA

# INTRODUCTION

As early as 1948 ties were established between British intelligence and South African 'Special Branch' officials, motivated by the mutual perceptions of a war against communism. Prior to 1960, when white South Africans voted in a referendum to become a republic, intelligence was supplied by Britain's MI5 and subsequently MI6. This cooperation led, in 1963, to the formation of South Africa's Republican Intelligence under Colonel Hendrik van den Bergh. The necessity of establishing a specialist intelligence unit became apparent after the 1960 Sharpeville massacre and the decision by the African National Congress (ANC) and the Communist Party (SACP) to form a military wing and commence armed struggle against the apartheid government. After 1961, South Africa now a republic, cooperation continued between South Africa, Britain's intelligence services and the Central Intelligence Agency. The arrest of Nelson Mandela on 5 August 1962 was as a result of a tip-off of Mandela's whereabouts by a CIA operative, Donald Rickard, to the South African Special Branch. In July 1962 the South African Defence Force (SADF) established a full military intelligence capability under General Retief who had aspirations of creating his own Central Intelligence Bureau. He failed in this regard, the prime minister, B. J. Vorster, preferring to allocate resources to his fellow Second World War Koffiefontein prisoner, Hendrik van den Bergh, the head of Republican Intelligence (RI)

'Prime Evil', Eugene de Kock.

The Black Sash was an anti-apartheid movement that sprang up in the 1950s. (*An Illustrated Dictionary of South African History*)

The six-foot-four Hendrik van den Bergh rapidly rose through the ranks of the security services. From colonel, at the age of forty- nine, after the conviction of Mandela and others in the Rivonia trial he became the youngest brigadier in the South African Police (SAP). In 1966 he became a major-general and in 1968 lieutenant-general when he set up the successor to Republican Intelligence, the Bureau for State Security (BOSS). '*Lang*' ('long') Hendrik, as he was known because of his height, was born in Vredefort in the Orange Free State in November 1914. In 1942 he was interred in the Koffiefontein camp alongside the man who was to become prime minister, John Vorster, for his suspected membership of a militant saboteur group linked to the pro-Nazi Ossewabrandwag ('ox wagon sentinels'). Lang Hendrik van den Bergh wielded his power through his lieutenants in the security forces. Feared and respected by his men, they would go to any length for him, "even to kill," so he said. Murder, elimination and 'removal' became the tools of trade of those who reported to him; blame for many of the atrocities committed by the death squads could be laid at his door.

A British diplomat described him: "The head of the new Bureau is clever ... He suffers from a megalomania and infallibility complex (his staff fawn over his lightest remark): this could be dangerous, particularly when combined with lieutenants who appear to be more remarkable for toughness and dedication than for the niceties of the law".[1] The operatives came from many sources: ex-Rhodesian soldiers with experience in fighting insurgents, members of Koevoet ('crowbar')—a paramilitary arm of the SAP that operated in Ovamboland against SWAPO (South West Africa People's Organization) and their allies, the MPLA (People's Movement for the Liberation of Angola), ex-policemen, *askaris* ('turned' activists who killed for their new masters),

The townships in many cases were little more than ghettos. This is Alexandra township in the northeastern suburbs of Johannesburg. (Robin Binckes)

members of the Recces (Reconnaissance Commandos, South Africa's special forces), mercenaries, gangsters and convicted criminals.

From 1969 to 1994 death squads operated throughout the country, and outside South Africa's borders. These agencies included BOSS (Bureau of State Security), Military Intelligence, the Security Police, the Regional Security Police, Vlakplaas, South African Medical Services, Civil Cooperation Bureau (CCB), and others.

The death squads operated mainly as autonomous units but at times worked in cooperation or partnership with one or another. Despite at times being partners in crime, there was intense rivalry and competition between the agencies, filtering down from the higher echelons of command as those at the top jostled for political and territorial power.

These teams who killed and maimed perceived enemies of the state operated under the overall umbrella of General Lang Hendrik van den Bergh. Some of the operatives were killers and killed because that is what they enjoyed doing: these were callous thugs. Many were soldiers who genuinely saw themselves fighting a war against communism.

Koevoet on operations in Ovamboland, South West Africa. (Attie Hattingh via Leon Beizuidenhout)

Koevoet trackers running on the spoor of SWAPO guerrillas in Ovamboland. (Attie Hattingh via Leon Beizuidenhout)

This book covers some of the killings by the organizations mentioned above, but by no means all. Some we will never know about. Many victims simply disappeared and today, despite efforts by the Truth and Reconciliation Commission, many cases are unsolved while others have never been exposed.

The generals lied to the politicians and the generals' foot soldiers did the bidding of the generals. How much did the politicians really know? We know of State President P. W. Botha's involvement in issuing orders to the generals to carry out illegal acts. We would be naïve to assume that those we are aware of were the only ones. If the president was involved, what of his cabinet? To claim that they were unaware is either an admission of incompetence or complicity.

*

By 2002, everyone in South Africa had heard of Vlakplaas, home of the death squads, but few knew anything about it. I was fascinated by the story, and the opportunity to learn more about it was catapulted into reality when the man who was to become my son-in-law, Jacques Pauw, visited me in Johannesburg and announced one Sunday morning: "You want to visit Vlakplaas, Rob? Come, let's go. I'll take you there."

Jacques, an investigative journalist at that time, was the man who at great risk to his own life exposed the existence of Vlakplaas in 1989 by breaking the story in the liberal Afrikaans newspaper *Vrye Weekblad*. There were few, if any, who knew more about Vlakplaas than Jacques, the author of three books on the subject—*In the Heart of the Whore, In the Heart of Darkness* and *Dances With Devils*—and a TV documentary, *Prime Evil,* under his belt. Two hours later Jacques and I were driving through the sleepy suburb of Erasmia on the outskirts of Pretoria, a popular residential suburb for Indian people being adjacent to Laudium, historically an Indian township. In the apartheid era, Erasmia was very much an Afrikaner suburb. Things have changed. We headed east on a dirt road for a few kilometres.

"There it is," said Jacques, indicating expansively the rolling hills of the Skurweberg. "There's Vlakplaas."

I could see splashes of red, the sun glinting off the tin roofs of the farmsteads. Vlakplaas looked like any other farm in the area. I am not sure what I expected but certainly not the air of normality that I experienced. We swung onto a dirt road leading to a locked gate in a security fence. There was no sign of life. From the direction of the buildings ahead came the sound of dogs barking. Large dogs. We rattled the gate to arouse some attention but everything remained still except for the barking dogs.

"Doesn't look like we can get in?" I said.

Vlakplaas, nestling peacefully in the hills outside Pretoria. (Robin Binckes)

Jacques shrugged and turned back to the car. "I'm not sure who lives here now but it looks like the farm is inhabited. But whoever does live here appears to be out. Sorry, Rob. We'll have to try again some other time."

"Someone's coming," I said. A young barefoot boy in shorts, aged about ten, was walking toward the gate. Three large ridgebacks bounded playfully beside him.

"*Môre oom,*" (Good morning uncle) the boy said.

"*Môre seun. Is jou pa hier? Ons wil 'n bietjie kuier,*" (Good morning, son. Is your father here? We want to visit) said Jacques.

"*Wil oom Vlakplaas besoek?*" (Does uncle want to visit Vlakplaas?)

"*Ja, seker,*" (Yes, definitely) said Jacques.

"*Oom jammer. My pa is nie op die oomblik hier nie. Hy is by die kerk. Maar as jy Vlakplaas will besoek moet jy hierdie telefoon nommer bel en toestemming van die regering kry.*" (Sorry uncle. My father is not here now. He is at church. But if you wish to visit Vlakplaas you must phone this number and get permission from the government.) The boy handed a piece of paper through the fence. I glanced down. It was a Pretoria number. Disappointed, Jacques and I returned to the car and headed back to Johannesburg.

"Well, Rob. You have a phone number. Give it a try, but I'm sure you'll get bounced around by bureaucrats—up to you."

Having recently qualified as a historical tour guide, I was anxious to expand my knowledge and places to take people to and felt that Vlakplaas would be an exciting destination. Accordingly, a few days later, I called the number. An official from the Department of Public Works answered immediately. I explained that the young boy at Vlakplaas had given me the number and that I felt it was important that the story of Vlakplaas should be shared and not forgotten. The man on the other end of the line listened.

"Email me an outline what you have just told me and I will come back to you," he said.

My heart sank knowing full well what dealing with a government department entailed. I sent the email. Within twenty-four hours I had a response from the Department of Public Works agreeing to my request.

I telephoned the Pretoria number again. "How will I get in?" I asked.

"Phone this number and speak to Louis Smit. He is the caretaker at Vlakplaas. He lives there with his family. He will let you in."

"How will he know that you have agreed?" I asked.

"The fact that you have his number means that we have given it to you and therefore we have given permission."

The next day, after phoning Louis Smit, I was back at Vlakplaas on my own. Louis Smit, a tall, grey-haired, fit and good-looking Afrikaner with startling blue eyes met me at the gate. He greeted me warmly as he firmly shook my hand. Over coffee he gave me his assurance that I could bring visitors to the farm and that he would cooperate in every way he could. I asked him how it was that he lived on the farm and he told me his story.

During the peak of the apartheid years, 1979 to 1993, Louis and his wife had lived in Canada where he had a printing business. He returned to South Africa in 1994, wishing to buy a farm. After looking at a number of farms along the Hennops river, he came across Vlakplaas and despite the fact that the farm was unoccupied and rundown, Louis wanted it. The farm had been trashed by vagrants, windows were broken, doors hung off hinges and the garden was completely overgrown. After discovering that the farm was owned by the government and administered by the Department of Public Works, he approached them to buy the farm. When they refused, because of its historical importance, Louis offered to live rent-free on the farm as the caretaker and renovate the farm buildings and maintain them at his own expense. This was agreed and Louis and his family moved in in 1996. I looked around. The lawns were neatly cut. Roses and daffodils grew in manicured flowerbeds. There were no broken windows and the buildings looked well maintained. We walked down to the Hennops river. The setting was idyllic.

"Here are the bones of the pigs that they killed when they tested out the bomb to kill Dirk Coetzee," he said as he scuffed with his shoe at some white bones half buried in the ground.

The banks of the Hennops river at the bottom of Vlakplaas where the pig's head was blown up in the rehearsal for sending the bomb to Dirk Coetzee. (Robin Binckes)

"*Ja,*" said Louis. "I can tell you a lot about Vlakplaas. Even about Eugene de Kock. I was here when the TRC [Truth and Reconciliation Commission] visited with de Kock. He and I prayed together. I often have visits from people who want to visit because they served here with death squads. Of course they don't say much but I know why they come." He pointed to the foundations of a building. "When I first saw the farm all the buildings were standing. But after I indicated interest, some of the buildings were destroyed ... such as these. This was the VIP quarters where the generals and other bigwigs stayed when they flew out from Pretoria to party with the guys at Vlakplaas—then they said they never knew anything about Vlakplaas." He grinned cynically and shook his head.

"This room here," he pointed at the window of a room in the main house. "This was the armoury and the room where they made the bomb that killed Bheki Malangeni. And over here," he pointed at more foundations, "these were police cells where they would torture their victims and turn them into askaris. Imagine being a general paying a visit and sitting here on the *stoep* [verandah] enjoying a gin and tonic. And maybe even a slice of lemon and watching the sun go down over there. The sound of the Hennops river down below and then, for added entertainment, the sounds of the victims being tortured right over here?" he said.

The main house at Vlakplaas. The room on the right was the armoury where the bomb that killed Bheki Malangeni was assembled. (Robin Binckes)

We walked past the main house to a small outbuilding. "This was a cell where they used to apply the helicopter treatment to turn their victims." He opened the door and in the gloom indicated three steel hooks in the concrete ceiling. "Here they would do the helicopter by suspending their victim from the hook, either upside down or right way up, bend their legs under them and put a wooden stick behind the knees, cover their heads with an inner car tube and hit them as they slowly turned. Then just before they passed out they would take a burning stick and shove it up their anus."

We walked out into the sunlight. The day suddenly felt very cold despite the sun beating down on us.

"This was the radio room," said Louis, pointing at another small outbuilding ... "and this was Eugene de Kock's office." He indicated a cement, rondaval-shaped building. "Up there is the helicopter pad where the generals who never knew about this place used to land. I've put a cross on it to keep the evil spirits away ... and those foundations you see there," he pointed to a concrete slab about fifteen metres square, "was the computer room where all the details of Operation Vula, the ANC's secret fallback plan, were kept, in case the CODESA [Convention for a Democratic South Africa] talks failed. De Kock was one of the few who had a key. Those buildings up there," he said, pointing to a row of red-brick buildings with bars on the windows that looked like a hybrid of a military barrack and a prison, "was where the askaris stayed."

We walked over to another building with an open area in front covered with shade cloth. Against a perimeter wall were two built-in *braai* (barbeque) areas, each some three or four metres wide. "This was their entertainment area. De Kock had a snooker table in the house, but this is where his men sat and did their daily admin. Over there," he pointed to a gazebo-type structure, "is where the dancing girls would perform, collected from the Polaris Hotel in Erasmia. Of course, there were three things readily available: drugs, sex and booze, all paid for by you and me, the taxpayers. That's the braai area." He pointed at the smaller braai. "And right next to that braai, while they were braaing meat, they could burn the bodies of their victims on the other braai. Takes seven hours for a body to burn and to turn to ash; the last parts to go are the buttocks and flanks. Then the remains would be disposed of in the Hennops."

I shivered as I looked at the giant human braai. (Eugene de Kock, however, categorically denies that anyone was ever burned at Vlakplaas.) I looked at the hill behind the buildings and noticed another wooden cross on the top of the hill. "That looks like it marks a grave?" I asked.

"*Ja*. It does. That's the grave of one of the askaris that de Kock had murdered. Brian Ngqulungu. They murdered him and then gave him an official police funeral."

Over the next few months Louis and I would meet for coffee and we developed a friendship that prevailed despite his attempts to convert me to his radical form of

The grave of Brian Ngqulunga who was murdered by his colleagues on de Kock's orders. (Robin Binckes)

The entrance to Vlakplaas. (Robin Binckes)

Christianity and despite his equally radical racial views. With Louis' consent I began to take visitors on tours to Vlakplaas. In the beginning Louis would make an appearance and talk to the guests and show them around. This ended when a group of journalists showed more interest in the story of Louis and his family than in the story of Vlakplaas. Thereafter, Louis seldom showed himself. After a few months of visiting the farm with guests, Louis trusted me sufficiently to give me my own gate key. I could come and go as I pleased.

Vlakplaas is a secluded 100-acre farm situated in the Skurweberg mountains on the outskirts of Erasmia, a Pretoria suburb along the banks of the Hennops river. It is well hidden from the public eye but close enough to Pretoria for helicopter access by generals and other high-ranking government officials.

The South African Police purchased Vlakplaas in 1979 as a secret hideout for a handful of white policemen and askaris to carry out clandestine operations against people identified as enemies of the state. The farm was the brainchild of Brigadier Johan Viktor who had learned in Rhodesia that captured soldiers could be 'turned" and used against their former comrades. 'Askari' was the term used to describe the policemen, mainly black, who had been members of one of the liberation movements such as the African National Congress (ANC), Pan Africanist Congress (PAC),

Azanian People's Organization (AZAPO) and others. Once captured by the Vlakplaas operatives, they would be brought to Vlakplaas, tortured (if needed) and 'turned' into askaris who would then be sent back to places like Soweto to carry out murder and atrocities against their own people. They became highly effective, as their victims would be unaware of their change of allegiance.

As early as 1963 South African Police colonel Att Spengler had first tried the technique of 'turning' ANC operatives into askaris at a police farm at Rietvlei, south of Pretoria.

The operatives at Vlakplaas operated from 1979 to 1994 during which time their role changed from carrying out assassinations and killings to fighting organized crime in Hillbrow, a cosmopolitan suburb of downtown Johannesburg notorious for illicit diamond-dealing and drugs. From fighting organized crime in Hillbrow, they became *the* organized crime of Johannesburg, involved in illegal arms-running and destabilizing the country in the build-up to the first democratic elections of 1994. It was Vlakplaas that became the shadowy, notorious 'Third Force'.

Eugene de Kock's office at Vlakplaas. (Robin Binckes)

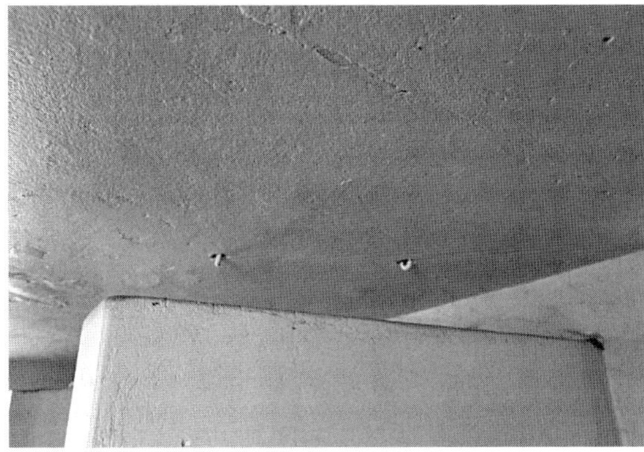

Hooks and chains in the ceilings where victims were suspended and beaten. This was denied by one of the ex-Vlakplaas operatives: "We used the hooks to dry biltong." (Robin Binckes)

Askari accommodation at Vlakplaas, a hybrid of barracks and a prison. (Robin Binckes)

# 1. APARTHEID, WIND OF CHANGE AND *ROOI GEVAAR*

After the formation of the Union of South Africa in 1910, in 1913 the first Land Act allocated a total of 7.2 percent of the surface area of South Africa to 90 percent of the population. The whites received 92.8 percent. The news of this impending act led to the formation of the South African Native National Congress, the first political organization for black people in South Africa. For the first time a group of black men—Saul Msane, Josiah Gumede, John Dube, Sol Plaatjie and Pixlie Ka Isaka Seme—banded together to provide black people with a voice to protest against the passing into law of the iniquitous act.

The 7.2 percent of land allocated to black people was extended in 1923 to 13.5 percent. That year the name of the organization was changed to the African National Congress which, together with other liberation movements, finally achieved their

Founders of South African Native National Congress, 1912. From left: Thomas Mapike, Rev Walter Rubusana, Rev John Dube, Saul Msane and Sol Plaatjie.

goal of universal suffrage in 1994. In 1948 the right-wing National Party was voted into power in a country where only 10 percent of the population, the whites, was allowed to vote. The 'Nats' immediately began to introduce a total of 148 laws under the umbrella of *apartheid* (separateness). Each of these laws was designed to entrench white supremacy. Discrimination had existed in southern Africa since the 1600s with the advent of the first Europeans. Some of the laws introduced by the Dutch in the 1700s were perpetuated by the British in the 1800s and then again by the white governments in the twentieth century. After 1948 everyone in South Africa was classified by colour. White people were referred to as 'Europeans' (with all the privileges). Black, coloured (mixed race) and Indian people were referred to as 'Non- Europeans' (with very few rights). They were not allowed to own land or to vote. One of the more visible manifestations of apartheid was the Separate Amenities Act, where every aspect of life was segregated. Signs on park benches loudly proclaimed EUROPEANS ONLY; there weren't any for non-whites as they were not allowed into parks.

This extended through to entrances to public places, counters in shops and post offices, railway carriages, buses, toilets, telephone booths and drycleaners. The Sports Act ensured that black, coloured and Indian people could not play sport against whites. Black, coloured and Indian people were not allowed to be included in any national team and blacks were not allowed into the stadiums to watch whites play sport. Further examples were the Mixed Marriages Act where whites and non-whites

Nationalists D. F. Malan and J. B. M. Herzog, architects of apartheid and later prime ministers, seen here in 1919.

J. G. Strijdom, D. F. Malan and P. O. Sauer celebrate the National Party's victory at the polls in 1948. (D. F. Malan Collection)

were not allowed to marry, the Immorality Act where sex between people of different races was illegal and punishable by five years' imprisonment, the Bantu Education Act where black people were assured of an inferior education and the dreaded pass laws that forced every black male over the age of sixteen to carry an identification document known as a pass. Caught without it or out of the area stipulated in the pass without the written permission of the police or the local magistrate or his employer was a criminal offence. The Group Areas Act forced non-Europeans to live in areas designated for them. Only blacks with jobs were allowed to be in a 'white' area.

One of the major factors in the story of South Africa was the almost pathological fear of communism, the *Rooi Gevaar,* the red danger. On 17 July 1950, the two-year-old nationalist government of the Union of South Africa introduced the Suppression of Communism Act. At the same time the U.S. entered the McCarthy era where thousands of innocent people were accused of supporting communism, mostly without any shred of evidence. In June 1950 the Korean War broke out and UN troops, primarily American, but also including, among others, British, Australian and South African, were sent to assist South Korea in the war against the Communist North. In 1961 the world teetered on the brink of global conflagration with the failed Bay of Pigs invasion of Cuba led by the CIA, followed in 1962 by the Cuban missile crisis, followed by the Vietnam War. All these events fuelled Western paranoia.

In South Africa, the bogeyman of communism in the West was like manna from heaven for the apartheid government. Those who demanded equal rights were now labelled communist. Communism was illegal and anyone caught and prosecuted as a communist was considered by most whites to be the most evil villain imaginable. The lines between communism and democracy became extremely blurred. Because the South African government was seen by the West to be anti-communist, the iniquitous apartheid laws initially barely aroused wrist-slapping indignation, principally from the United Kingdom and the U.S.

In the 1950s Britain began to grant independence to its African colonies. In 1957 the Gold Coast became independent Ghana. In 1960 the Belgians granted independence to the Congo and Britain to Nigeria. To the apartheid South African government Africa must have appeared to be a collapsing house of cards.

On a visit to South Africa in 1960, in a speech to the South African parliament, in which he referred to the wind of change blowing across the continent, British prime minister Harold Macmillan made it clear that the time had come for independence to be granted to British colonies to the north of South Africa. He also made it clear that there were many South African policies that were unacceptable to the British government. The listening MPs met the speech with a stony silence.

Following Macmillan's 'wind of change' speech, in short order nineteen African countries were granted independence by their colonial masters, Britain, France and Belgium. The wind of change had become a hurricane, sometimes with deadly effect. On 21 March 1960 South African Police opened fire on a group of protestors at Sharpeville, a township some fifty kilometres south of Johannesburg. A peaceful demonstration against the pass laws ended with sixty-nine people shot dead and 183 wounded. Mandela, on hearing the news said, "We have knocked on the door for so long. It hasn't opened. It is time to blow it down." The government banned both the ANC and the PAC on 8 April 1960. The ANC, which up to that time had been following Gandhi's teachings of peaceful resistance, changed direction. The formation of the Pan Africanist Congress, a rival militant group, on 6 April 1959 under Robert Sobukwe was attracting frustrated members of the ANC and, coupled with the Sharpeville shooting, persuaded the ANC to take up arms. It formed a coalition with the Communist Party of South Africa which was predominantly white and together they launched the joint military wing known as Mkhonto WeSizwe (Spear of the Nation) or 'MK' with Nelson Mandela as its commander in chief. The military goal was the overthrow of the apartheid government, known as Operation *Mayibuywa* (to come home).

MK carried out its first military attack against the government on 16 December 1961. The 16th of December is a day revered by the Afrikaners and remembered every year with church services and a public holiday, as on that day in 1838, 464 Boers (Afrikaners) defeated a Zulu army of 20,000 at Blood River, killing between 3,000 and 10,000 Zulu warriors without losing a single man. This contributed significantly to the belief that God was on the side of the Afrikaner and thus the day became known as 'The Day of the Vow', subsequently changed to the 'Day of the Covenant'. It was no accident that this date was chosen by MK to launch the armed struggle.

In 1961 MK purchased the 28-acre farm Liliesleaf on the northern outskirts of Johannesburg as a secret hideout where the communists and the ANC could meet and plan the military overthrow of the country. The money to purchase the farm was provided by Moscow. Acting on a tip-off from a CIA operative, Donald Rickart, in 1962 the police arrested Nelson Mandela near Howick in Natal. He was charged with leaving the country illegally and inciting a labour strike. He was found guilty and sentenced to five years' imprisonment on Robben Island.

Despite Mandela's imprisonment, the meetings plotting the overthrow of the government continued at Liliesleaf. On 11 July 1963 most of the other conspirators were arrested at Liliesleaf Farm when they were caught red-handed planning Operation Mayibuya: the police found them with plans for making forty-nine tons of ammonium nitrate, eighteen tons of black powder for manufacturing gunpowder, timing devices, landmines and hand grenades. They also found a sixty-two-page document entitled 'How to be a Good Communist. Written by Nelson Mandela'. Mandela was brought out of prison and charged with sabotage. He became 'Accused number one' in the subsequent trial, known as the Rivonia Trial. He and seven others were found guilty of sabotage and sentenced to life imprisonment.

Farther afield, of what was later termed the frontline states, Kenya became the first of these countries to benefit from the wind of change, becoming independent from Great Britain in 1963. Tanganyika and Zanzibar became Tanzania in 1964, Northern Rhodesia became Zambia in the same year, followed in 1965 by the protectorate of Bechuanaland bordering South Africa becoming Botswana. Mozambique, South Africa's immediate neighbour to the east, was already feeling the first cramps of a guerrilla campaign that would ultimately topple the Portuguese in 1974.

South Africa's neighbour to the north, Rhodesia, had hit a stumbling block that turned out to be a wall on its path to independence. Prime Minister Ian Smith, a former RAF fighter pilot shot down in the Second World War was told by the Labour prime minister Harold Wilson that Rhodesia would only be granted independence when democratic elections—i.e. 'one man one vote'—were held. To hasten the process, Ndabaningi Sithole and his deputy Robert Mugabe of the Zimbabwean African National Union (ZANU) joined forces with Joshua Nkomo and his Zimbabwean African People's Union (ZAPU) to launch a war of liberation against Smith and his white government, commencing in July 1964 and continuing for fifteen years. After futile and fiery negotiations, in an attempt to hold onto minority white rule, Ian Smith and his government unilaterally declared independence (UDI) from Britain on 11 November 1965 (another date specifically and unsubtly chosen). The war began in earnest on 28 April 1966 when three groups of Zimbabwe African National Liberation Army (ZANLA, ZANU's military wing) insurgents entered Rhodesia from Zambia with the aim of attacking power lines and white farmsteads. The following year MK and PAC insurgents teamed up with the Zimbabwe People's Revolutionary Army (ZIPRA, ZAPU's military wing) near the Victoria Falls and clashed with Rhodesian security forces in the Zambezi valley. This was the excuse the South African government needed to get involved.

South African Police helicopters (aka SAAF helicopters) and personnel, including helicopter pilots, saw action in the Zambezi valley of Rhodesia under the guise of combating South African guerrillas.

As the war escalated and the world turned its back on Rhodesia, South Africa got sucked into the political and military quagmire by providing Ian Smith, and what had become an illegal regime, tacit and overt support. Given the excuse that her borders were under threat and conscious of the eyes of the rest of the world on Rhodesia, South Africa was well aware that she too could become the butt of sanctions that had been placed by the international community on Rhodesia. South Africa could not send in her army to assist Smith so they did the next best thing and, in 1967, members of the South African Police were sent into Rhodesia to fight shoulder to shoulder with the Rhodesian army, along with South African Air Force (SAAF) helicopters and pilots rebranded as SAP.[1]

After the sentencing and imprisonment of Nelson Mandela and other leaders of the resistance movement, unrest and terrorist attacks diminished. For the next decade the apartheid regime ruled with an iron fist.

In April 1975 the last American troops left Saigon, signalling an end to the Vietnam War. The following year the nationalist government of South Africa decided that black high-school children were to be taught four subjects in Afrikaans: mathematics, biology, history and physical science. After a period of stayaways and class boycotts by Soweto students, events came to a head on the morning of 16 June 1976 when nineteen-year-old Tsiietsie Mashinini led a protest march from the Morris Isaacson High School. The plan was to march to the Orlando soccer stadium where other schools would join them in a protest meeting. They never arrived at the stadium. A few hundred children left Morris Isaacson High School at 0815. By the time they had marched five and a half kilometres, there were more than ten thousand singing, chanting students. A police roadblock in Vilakazi Street then confronted the march. The violence which had been bubbling

A forced removal into the 'bantustans', the so-called black homelands. This one is taking place in the Western Transvaal in 1984. (Paul Weinberg)

beneath the surface began to boil over. Tensions were taut as rocks were thrown, a police dog was set alight and the police opened fire on the students. As they did so, a thirteen-year-old schoolboy, Hector Pieterson spotted his sister, seventeen-year-old Antoinette, as one of the marchers and ran to join her. He was hit by police bullets and fell dying. He was picked up and carried in the arms of one of the student marchers, Mbuyisa Makhubo. Sam Nzima, a photographer for *The World* newspaper, took a picture of the dying boy in the arms of Makhubo and the picture was flashed around the world and the name Hector Pieterson became synonymous with 16 June.

Sam Nzima's famous photograph of the dying Hector Pieterson in the June 1976 students' uprising is seen here blown up and framed at the Hector Pieterson Memorial, Soweto (Robin Binckes).

From that moment Soweto exploded. Five hundred people died over the next two days, many of them children. Buildings were set on fire, buses and trucks torched and more innocent people died. The violence quickly spread to other townships. The government declared a state of emergency: among other measures no gathering of more than three people could take place. Armoured SAP vehicles moved in to patrol the townships. For two years the government managed to keep a lid on the boiling pot. During that period between 1976 and 1978 it is estimated that more than twenty thousand youths left the country and joined one of the liberation movements in exile to be trained as freedom fighters, or terrorists, depending on one's views. Many received training in communist countries such as China, Cuba, the USSR and other Eastern bloc states. The boy who had led the march, Tsietsie Mashinini, also went into hiding and joined the youth in exile, in August 1976.

In 1978, at Moscow's urging, the man who was to succeed Nelson Mandela and become president of South Africa, Thabo Mbeki, together with MK chief of staff Joe Slovo, ANC president Oliver Tambo, MK commander Joe Modise and SACP assistant general-secretary Chris Hani, all in exile at the time, visited Vietnam and met with former Viet Cong and Vietnamese army delegates, academics, priests and other members of civil society. Their visit culminated in a meeting with the legendary strategist General Vo Nguyen Giap, former commander of the North Vietnamese army.

The visit to Vietnam changed the thinking of the ANC high command and resulted in a document entitled 'Summarized Theses on Our Strategic Line' which was approved by the ANC national executive committee. It was then published in August 1989 as *The Green Book: Lessons From Vietnam.*[2] This in turn became *The Four Pillars of Revolution*, the blueprint for the ANC's struggle in South Africa from 1978 to 1994.

The four pillars were the all-round activity of the underground structures of the ANC, the united mass action of the people (mass mobilization), the armed offensive and the international drive to isolate South Africa.[3]

*Left*: Oliver Tambo in 1983. (Nationaal Archief NL)

*Below*: Nelson Mandela (extreme left) with Algerian leaders, on a visit in 1962.

# 2. ENTER BOSS

In an attempt to counter the activities of MK, in 1969 the South African prime minister, B. J. Vorster, established the Bureau for State Security (BOSS) under the leadership of General 'Lang' Hendrik van den Berg. Van den Berg was some years later to testify to a commission of inquiry: "I can tell you here today, not for your records, but I can tell you I have enough men to commit murder if I tell them to kill ... Those are the kind of men I have. And if I wanted to do something like that to protect the security of the State nobody would stop me. I would stop at nothing."

Vorster had been minister of justice prior to being elected prime minister after the assassination of Dr Verwoed in 1966. The process of eliminating opponents to the apartheid government began under van den Berg's command. It was believed to be far more cost-effective and simpler to go into a township and murder victims identified as enemies of the state than to go the tedious route of prosecuting them through the courts. In effect van den Bergh's lieutenants became judge, jury and executioner.

To achieve his goals van den Bergh used any means at his disposal. This is evidenced by the strange relationship that he established in the 1960s with Charlie

B. J. Vorster, seen here in 1960. (*Ons Eerste Halfeeu 1910–1960*)

Founder of BOSS, 'Lang' Hendrik van den Berg, in 1976.

Richardson, the notorious leader of a London gang that fought the Kray twins for control of the London underworld. Richardson carried out assignments in London on behalf of Republican Intelligence, which included robbery of address cards, notebooks, pictures and documents from the Anti-Apartheid Movement offices, the Zimbabwe People's Union offices and Amnesty International. Richardson was sentenced to twenty-five years in prison in 1966 in what became known as the 'torture trial', referring to Richardson's favorite method of punishing his underworld victims. No matter how unsavory the characters were, as long as they carried out van den Bergh's wishes, he employed them.

In 1969, according to Gordon Winter, a BOSS agent, Lang Hendrik van den Berg received information that a plan was being hatched to assist Nelson Mandela escape from Robben Island where he was imprisoned. Winter infiltrated the plotters and became involved in the planning, aiming to hijack the operation. Mandela was to be given a revolver loaded with blanks which he could use if the police arrived at the scene where he was to be picked up by a light aircraft and flown off the island. The revolver would provide the police the excuse to shoot Mandela. After Mandela had been killed, the blanks would be substituted with live ammunition. The plan came to naught due mainly to the reluctance of the pilot of the aircraft to go through with it.

Contact with the CIA was always via BOSS. It was BOSS who initiated the request for arms and ammunition for anti-communist forces, such as Jonas Savimbi's UNITA in Angola.

BOSS agents identified Peter Hain, a British Liberal Party MP, as a target to discredit due to his anti-apartheid stance and encouragement of the sports boycott against South Africa. In 1972 a letter bomb was sent to Hain which failed to explode and in 1975 an elaborate plan was put into place to frame him in connection with the theft of £490 pounds from the Putney branch of Barclays Bank by a Hain lookalike hired by BOSS for the project.

BOSS carried out assassinations of identified anti-apartheid activists. As early as 1969 Brigadier W. A. L. du Toit of BOSS was involved in the production of explosive devices intended for unknown victims selected by BOSS as targets. Brigadier Willem Schoon applied for amnesty from the TRC for the abduction, arrest and killing of two ANC combatants in July 1972. In February 1974 BOSS agents sent a letter bomb to Abram Tiro, an academic and anti-apartheid activist who had fled South Africa and was in hiding in Botswana. The bomb exploded, killing Tiro. Twelve days later John Dube, the ANC representative in Zambia, was killed by a parcel bomb.

Not to be outdone, in 1971, and seeing themselves as custodians of the security of South Arica, soon after the formation of BOSS, the Defence Force created 1 Reconnaissance Commando "to inflict maximum disruption on the enemy of the state by means of special activities". Soon after 2 Recce was established and after the Soweto uprising a decision was taken to establish a group specializing in the use of black soldiers who had been trained in guerilla warfare. In December 1976 fifteen men under the command of Major P. J. 'Joe' Verster were sent to Rhodesia for training.

In 1978, 4 Recce was established in the Cape and, in 1980, 3 Recce was created to incorporate the substantial number of Rhodesian special forces soldiers, mainly SAS and Selous Scouts, who had immigrated to the republic after the establishment of Zimbabwe. In 1980 Major-General Loots, the commanding officer of the Special Forces, travelled to Rhodesia to personally screen potential recruits. This led to the establishment of Delta 40 or D40 under the command of ex-SAS Garth Barrett. D40 was composed almost totally of ex- Rhodesians. In 1981 D40 was renamed Barnacle. Barnacle was to play a major role in destabilizing the counties immediately adjacent to South Africa, known as the front line states, in particular Zambia, Mozambique and Zimbabwe. In January 1981 members of Barnacle attacked three houses in Maputo, killing thirteen ANC activists and in July 1981 they assassinated Joe Gqabi, deputy head of ANC intelligence, in Harare, Zimbabwe.[1]

To destabilize Zimbabwe Barnacle members planted a massive bomb which destroyed more than R45 million worth of munitions and weapons. Its final external operation was the destruction of thirteen aircraft of the Zimbabwean air force at Gweru's Thornhill airbase in July 1982

By August 1982, Barnacle was also operating internally in urban counterinsurgency by disposing of 'unwanted individuals' during or after interrogation and dumping the bodies of their victims in the sea. Their victims included hundreds of SWAPO prisoners of war. In July 1986, with the non-Afrikaans-speaking ex-Rhodesians gone, Barnacle was redesignated the Civil Cooperation Bureau (CCB).[2]

Apart from the death squads operated by BOSS, Military Intelligence, Vlakplaas and the CCB, a culture of brutality existed among members of the SAP that led to the murder of many of their victims. Suspects were routinely tortured and beaten in an attempt to harvest information about the activities of MK. Two of these early victims were Ahmed Timol and Steve Biko. In 1971 Ahmed Timol died after falling from a tenth-floor window at the notorious John Vorster Square, police headquarters in Johannesburg.

Ahmed Timol on an ANC poster.

Timol was a Communist Party member, a member of MK and an anti-apartheid activist. He had lived in exile in London and had attended the Lenin Institute in Moscow before returning to South Africa and working underground for the ANC. Picked up by the security police, he was tortured before plunging to his death on 27 October 1971. The inquest found that he had committed suicide. His family worked tirelessly, never giving up, to establish the truth. In October 2017, forty-six years after his death, Judge Billy Mothle ruled that a witness, João Rodrigues, had lied at the two inquests held in 1972 and 2017 and that Rodriguez was an accomplice after the fact to murder and that Timol had been pushed from the window by security police after being savagely beaten.

Regional security police were also involved in assassinations and killing. Under Colonel Piet Goosen the Eastern Cape Security Police soon established a reputation for being one of the most brutal in their fight against the ANC. One such victim was Steve 'Bantu' Biko.

Biko, leader of the Black Consciousness movement, was tortured and beaten in Port Elizabeth by members of the Eastern Cape Security Branch. He had been kept manacled and naked for twenty days while Goosen interrogated him. He had not been allowed out of the cell during that period. He was assaulted frequently and was struck all over his body and head. Some of the blows to the head caused brain damage. Goosen claimed that Biko was a terrorist leader. A Port Elizabeth district surgeon, Dr Ivor Lang, was called in to examine Biko. When Lang arrived he found Biko lying on a mat and chained to a grill. During his examination of Biko he found bruises and lacerations, his movements uncoordinated and his speech slurred. Yet Lang wrote in his report that he found no evidence of abnormality or pathology on the patient.

Steve Biko.

Lang was called by Goosen again the next day and arrived with his superior, Benjamin Tucker. They found Biko lying on a mat soaked in urine. Again the report stated that there had been no change in Biko's condition. The next day a warder found Biko collapsed, frothing at the mouth, hyperventilating and glassy-eyed. Despite this Tucker gave his consent for Biko to be transported to Pretoria, some 1,200 kilometres away, without medical personnel or medical records. The semiconscious Biko was dumped naked into a police van and transported in that manner to Pretoria where he died.[3] When the minister of justice and the police, Jimmy Kruger, was informed of Biko's death he famously commented, "It leaves me cold."

Enemies of the state could be identified in what appeared as the most unlikely guises. The brutal murder of Robert and Jean Smit on the night of 22 November 1977 was found by the Truth and Reconciliation that members of the security forces killed the Smits. The details of the murders have never been proved but there was sufficient evidence available to lead the TRC to the conclusion that it was carried out by members of BOSS and their agents.[4]

The murders have never been solved but the trails lead back to Hendrik van den Bergh and BOSS founder members of 'Z Squad', a hit squad. Names that keep cropping up are Dries Verwey (who died of a heart attack, but who some claim was murdered), Roy Allen (who has recently returned to South Africa from Australia and who denies any involvement), Philip Freeman (who died after 'accidentally' being shot by his own weapon when he tripped over his dog, having gone outside his house to investigate a noise; before his death he denied any involvement) and Jack Widdowson.

Robert Smit, a rising star in the National Party.

Robert Smit was a glittering star in the National Party galaxy, having rapidly risen through the ranks. Many people believed that following the general election to be held on 30 November 1977, Smit would be appointed minister of finance in the nationalist government. He was a Rhodes scholar at Oxford University and had received a doctorate in economics from Stellenbosch University. He then served as South Africa's representative to the International Monetary Fund in Washington. When he returned to South Africa in January 1976 he took up a position as chief executive of Santam International, a company with links to the insurance giant, Santam. Smit and Dr Carel van Aswegan, Santam's chairman, owned between them 30 percent of the shares in the company. At the time of his death Santam International was heavily involved in 'sanctions busting', particularly in oil.[5] Smit had rented a house in Springs, a small mining town on the Rand, some forty kilometres east of Johannesburg where Smit was busy campaigning for the Springs seat on behalf of the National Party in the forthcoming election.

On the day before his death his secretary noticed a letter terminating his services at Santam International.[6] His daughter Liza Smit informed me that he had also been made to return his shares in Santam International. On the day of his murder Robert Smit spent the day at his electoral offices in Springs and had lunch with friends. His receptionist, Sarah Lombard, took a call from a man at 3.15 p.m. who announced himself as Mr McDougall and requested a meeting with Dr Smit that night. Sarah put the caller through to Dr Smit to make his own arrangements as she was unaware of any of his appointments that evening. After the call Smit recorded the name McDougall in his diary for the time 8 p.m.

That evening Robert Smit's wife, Jean, returned home from shopping soon after 6 p.m., driven by their driver Daniel Tshabalala. Daniel made himself supper in the kitchen while Jean relaxed in front of the TV in the living room. Daniel Tshabalala left the house a few minutes before 7 o'clock and she would have heard the door lock behind him. She called her husband's office sometime just before 8 o'clock and spoke to the receptionist and asked her to remind Dr Smit that his guests were soon due. It seems that as she put the phone down she sensed something or someone behind her and instinctively put up her right hand to protect herself. A shot was fired at close range from a .38 Webley pistol into the back of her head, a second shot struck her in the chest as she fell and a third hit her in her right thigh. The shot in her leg was fired from an Astra .32 revolver.[7] She was then stabbed fourteen times all over her body with a stiletto dagger.[8] Any one of the stab wounds would have been fatal.

Just before 8 p.m. Smit left his office for home carrying two files of documents. When he arrived home he parked in the street as there was a car in front of the garage. He was killed nearly two and a half hours after leaving his office. The time between leaving the office and being killed still remains a blank. Nobody knows where he was or whom he was with. There are many theories about the killings, none of which can be substantiated.

According to the *Cape Times*, after killing Jean Smit, the five assassins waited for Robert to arrive. They removed the bulb on the stoep so that Smit would not be able to see the shooters as he entered the house. Smit was silhouetted against the light, making a clear target when one assassin fired from the darkened stoep. He was shot in the neck and then at close range in the head. The bullet shattered his skull and splintered the bone. He was then stabbed with the stiletto dagger and his body dragged round the corner into the passage. The killers spraypainted the words RAU TEM in red on the wall and across the fridge.

However, another slightly different version of events is that Robert Smit was shot inside the house after he had entered the front door. A low wall divided the living room from the passage, behind which lay the body of Jean Smit that would have been masked from Smit's line of sight. As Smit opened the front door, one assassin appeared in front of him and another to his side. The .38 bullet fired from the Webley[9] pistol of the assassin in front of Smit hit him in the skull and the bullet from the assassin standing to the side of the door struck him in the neck. The two men, possibly assisted by a third, later dragged Smit's body round the corner into the house proper. From the blood on the floor that marked the spot where Smit fell, it would appear that Smit was still alive and bleeding and lay for some time where he had been shot before the killers dragged his body round the corner.

The spraypainted RAU TEM remained a mystery for years. It is recently believed to have been a code used by Lang Hendrik van den Bergh when recording killings carried out by the state. BOSS had secret quarters on an island in the Vaal Dam named Groot Eiland (large island) owned by Rand Afrikaans University and leased to BOSS on a ninety-nine-year lease. Some BOSS operations were conducted from the island. RAU TEM is an intialism for **R**andse **A**frikaanse **U**niversiteit **T**egnies **E**n **M**oord, or Rand Afrikaans University Technical & Murder.

According to a source who spoke to the *Cape Times* in 2012, he was one of the five who had killed the Smits. The source had known underworld connections in South Africa. The hit squad consisted of himself, an American, a Cuban named Virgilio Paz and known as Romero, a Mexican and McDougall. McDougall was the *nom de guerre* of the former BOSS operative, Phil Freeman.[10] The *Sunday News Journal*, Delaware, published an article by Joe Trento in which he stated that in 1973 BOSS and its Chilean counterpart, the National Intelligence Directorate (DINA), had established hit teams using CIA-trained, anti-Castro fanatics to undertake contract killings. The article tallied with the information provided by the *Cape Times* source.[11]

The next morning, the Smits' driver, Daniel Tshabalala, raised the alarm when he found the bodies of his murdered employers. The police responded immediately and sealed off the area, allowing no one into the crime scene ... except Gordon Winter who worked as a journalist for *The Citizen* newspaper—established as an illegal propaganda publication from secret government funds—and who was a BOSS spy and operative.

According to James Sanders in his book *Apartheid's Friends,* Winter recalled that his handler, Jacobus Johannes 'Koos' Kemp, called him into BOSS headquarters and told him that Smit had been killed by at least two assassins. Winter explained that at least one of the assassins was a specialist killer who had raised the gun above his victim's head before bringing it down in front of his body, with the bullets fired repeatedly as the gun travelled downward. This theory doesn't tally with the bullet wounds found in Smit.

The most likely theory is that the assassins were all part of BOSS. There was no need to bring in professional killers from overseas. They existed in-country. If there were overseas killers they were operating under BOSS instructions and with BOSS operatives. The names that keep coming to the fore are Phil Freeman (McDougall), Dries Verwey and Roy Allen. Allen, the only one of the three who is still alive, issued a statement denying his involvement and speculating how Verwey and Freeman could have carried out the assassination. Of all the BOSS operatives Roy Allen had the closest association with Robert Smit. His girlfriend Ida had once worked as Smit's secretary and Allen acknowledges that he had met Smit before.

He states:

> Killing the enemy—I expressly do not use the word 'murder'—was probably something that came easily for Delta Victor [Verwey]. He received the SA Police's highest medal for bravery for some operation in Zambia or Botswana. It was done in the commissioner's office, as no mention was made about it in dispatches. He was heavily involved in the Portuguese PIDE [secret police] effort in Mozambique against FRELIMO [liberation movement], and this was a no-holds-barred war by a desperate and cruel Portuguese military dictatorship. (I do not criticize his/the Portuguese actions, and I would have followed a similar course of action had I been involved at the time.)
>
> His other partner in the 'Smit affair' was most probably Phil Freeman. I have thought long and hard about the Smit murders since 1996 when the allegations of my involvement—as well as that of Phil and Verwey—arose in the SA media. The following is a possible set-out for what transpired:
>
> - Phil drives up from Cape Town and meets Verwey at a motel on the East Rand where a room is booked in a false name. He would have used his subsidized vehicle with false plates. This way, there would be no air ticket records, and Phil would have disconnected the speedometer on his BOSS-subsidized vehicle so as not to have to explain excessive mileage.

- Phil travels overnight, arriving mid-morning and sleeps for most of the day. Verwey arrives late afternoon, and they go over the final planning for the mission in the motel room, consuming takeaway food that Verwey had supplied. Verwey has a stolen car that they use for the mission, and he provides the weapon/s. (There would be no drinking before the 'ops'.)
- After completion of the mission, they return to the motel to shower and get rid of their bloodstained clothing. Both have one celebratory *dop* of whisky, and then Verwey drives the car to a remote area adjoining a black township on the West Rand where he torches the vehicle. Phil then drops him off at his 'official' vehicle safely parked somewhere in Springs or environs.
- Verwey goes back home to Pretoria and Phil drives back to Cape Town, arriving in the early hours—and phoning in sick to take the day off to rest. Phil would not have left the contaminated clothing in the stolen vehicle they set alight just in case it did not burn out properly. He would have taken it with him and stopped somewhere in the middle of the Karoo [arid semi-desert region in the northern Cape en route to Cape Town from Johannesburg]. He would have completely burnt it out with petrol, then stirred the ashes and burnt it again.

It was reported that Smit was in possession of certain information regarding massive corruption and money laundering that involved the minister of finance, Dr Nico Diedrichs, and other leading cabinet ministers and that he intended spilling the beans. He had to be stopped. The government denied any involvement in, or connection with, the Smit murders. Some years later one of the doyens of South African journalism, Allister Sparks, was tipped off by Mervyn Rees, an investigative journalist, about a conversation that he had had with a Supreme Court judge, Joe Ludof, at his home. Ludof had informed Rees of a "capital evacuation scheme" and that Dr Diedrichs had done a deal with the Union Bank of Switzerland where money siphoned off from gold sales would be deposited into a private account. He gave Rees the bank account number and Rees gave the bank account number to Allister Sparks. Sparks decided to check the authenticity of the account. He travelled to Zurich and visited the main branch of UBS bank. He filled in a deposit slip in his own name to deposit 50 Swiss francs into account 187.613LIE, the account number given to him by Rees. He handed it to a teller who stamped it and handed the receipt back to Sparks. The next day, to be sure, he repeated the process at the same bank, only this time he made the depositor Dr Nico Diedrichs, Pretoria, South Africa, and handed a 30 franc note for deposit. Again it was accepted. It was clear that the account existed. He then attempted to phone the retired head of UBS who refused to say anything that might besmirch the name of Nico Diedrichs.[12]

No arrests have ever been made in connection with the Smit murders. It is believed that Robert Smit, through his work with the IMF, had come across overseas bank accounts which would have implicated senior members of government in corruption and theft. He had on a number of different occasions talked about the fact that he was in possession of information that could bring down the government and that he intended exposing certain officials. It is not known who pulled the trigger but, metaphorically, the bullets were loaded by van den Burgh and manufactured by senior members of government. The TRC found that Robert and Jean Smit were killed by members of the security forces and that their deaths constituted a gross violation of human rights.

Rick Turner, a radical political scientist who had been married to a Muslim woman, experienced many acts of intimidation prior to his murder at the hands of BOSS on 8 January 1978: his motorbike had been set on fire, his car tyres slashed, a load of cement dumped on his doorstep and a bomb thrown into his house. He was killed while putting his two daughters to bed at 12.30 at night. He heard a knock on the front door and, curious to see who would be visiting at such late hour, put his head out of the window to see who it was. He was shot at point-blank range.[13] Phil Freeman of BOSS was named as one of the killers in the Truth and Reconciliation hearings.

The classic portrait of Rick Turner's daughter, Jann, with Eugene de Kock at the TRC hearings in 1997. Jann was thirteen when her father was gunned down in front of her. (George Hallett)

# 3. VLAKPLAAS AND 'PRIME EVIL'

In 1979, after getting embroiled in the infamous 'Information scandal', BOSS morphed into the South African Department of National Security after van den Berg had resigned the year before. It was against this background that the South African Police purchased a farm as a secret hideout and from where operations could be launched to stem the *Rooi Gevaar*. The farm was called Vlakplaas. Initially it was rented but finally purchased in 1981 to become the home to an anti-terrorist group of Section C10 of the South African Police under General Johan Coetzee. The purpose of the operatives on the farm was to capture ANC or PAC cadres and turn them into askaris "to fight terrorism with terrorism".

One of the cells at Vlakplaas where victims were given the 'helicopter' and 'the tube' torture treatments. (Robin Binckes)

**'Muldergate', the Information Scandal**
In the face of increasing world pressure to abandon the policy of apartheid, in 1977 the South African government established the Department of Information

under Dr Connie Mulder, leader of the National Party in the Transvaal and recognized as the most powerful figure in government after Prime Minister Vorster. Mulder convinced Vorster to agree to the setting up of a 'counter-offensive' through the media and if necessary by covert means. Mulder appointed the flamboyant Eschel Rhoodie to lead the offensive. Working hand in glove with BOSS's General van den Bergh, over a hundred secret projects were illegally funded through vast sums of money siphoned off from the 'special defence account' (used to secretly purchase arms). However, Rhoodie's grotesquely lavish life style soon raised eyebrows and, after investigations by local newspaperr the *Daily Mail* and *Sunday Express*, the scale of the misappropriation of taxpayers' money became apparent. Just a few of the illegally funded projects included:

- Funding of *The Citizen* newspaper.
- Launch of propaganda magazine *To The Point* in South Africa by Dutch publisher Hubert Jussen, funded by the department.
- Award of $10 million to U.S. publisher McGoff to buy *Washington Star*: bid failed.
- McGoff then 'purchased' his own paper, *Sacramento Union*, for Rhoodie.
- Attempt by Rhoodie to purchase *Investors' Chronicle* through fronts Stuart Pegg and David Abrahamson: failed.
- Establishment by Rhoodie of two advertising agencies, Club of Ten and The Committee for Fairness in Sport.
- Placement of pro-South African ads in *The Guardian, The Observer* and the *Daily Telegraph* in UK and *The New York Times, Washington Post*, the *Montreal Star* as well as newspapers in Australia, New Zealand, Holland and West Germany.
- Financing the movie *Golden Rendezvous* which failed dismally.
- Luxurious holidays in Europe, North America and the Indian Ocean islands for Rhoodie's friends and family.
- Rhoodie owned luxury apartments in Paris, upmarket Clifton in Cape Town and the jet-set holiday resort of Plettenberg Bay in the Cape, luxury homes in Pretoria, London and New York and a share in a South African game farm.

The scandal led to Vorster's resignation and the downfall of Connie Mulder as the man to succeed him, by Minister of Defence P. W. Botha. Rhoodie left South Africa in disgrace. After time in Ecuador and then France, he settled in the U.S. He died playing tennis in Atlanta on 17 July 1993.[1]

Eschel Rhoodie see here with Lang Hendrik van den Bergh in Paris, 1979 (*Apartheid's Friends* by James Sanders, published by John Murray Press, an imprint of Hodder & Stoughton)

C10 became a death squad proper. No stone was left unturned as C10 and other death squads honed their skills. Much of their art of torture and killing was learned from some of the most repressive regimes in the world, Argentina being one. In 1981 Alfredo Astiz, the most notorious torturer of political prisoners in Argentina, was posted to the Argentine embassy in Pretoria. Several seminars and workshops took place, attended by Argentinian security police and members of C10 where techniques were discussed and ideas exchanged.

Dirk Coetzee, the first commander at Vlakplaas, was appointed in August 1980. He was a fast-rising star in the SAP. Vlakplaas commanders had two things in common: all had undergone training at the SAP College in Pretoria and all had served in the counterinsurgency unit of the SAP in Rhodesia where they had learned their craft.

Coetzee had a small group of askaris under him that included Jeff Bosigo, Peter Kgoadi, Thabo Makgage, Steven Mbanda, Piet Mogai, Gladstone Mose, and Joe Mamasela (who became one of the most notorious killers), Brian Ngqulunga, Ernest Ramatlala and Almond Nofamelo. When Coetzee arrived at Vlakplaas he found the askaris in a sorry state. They drank heavily, smoked *dagga* (marijuana) and were poorly paid and badly treated. Coetzee motivated to have their salaries increased, gave them clothing allowances, put them on the SAP medical scheme and arranged firearm permits. Discipline was shocking.

*Above left*: P. W. Botha as minister of defence. A ruthless nationalist, he was not afraid to get his hands dirty. (*Wie is Wie in Suid-Afrika 1963*)

*Above right*: Griffiths Mxenge, stabbed multiple times by Dirk Coetzee's men. (*In the Heart of the Whore* by Jacques Pauw, published by Southern Book Publishers)

On 19 November 1981, in Durban, anti-apartheid activist and Human Rights lawyer Griffiths Mxenge who represented many banned ANC cadres, was murdered. Coetzee ordered his men, Joe Mamasela, Brian Ngqulunga, Almond Nofomela and David Tshikalanga to undertake the killing. The four askaris lured Mxenge to a sports stadium in Umlazi, the black township outside Durban. After poisoning his dog, they attacked Mxengu and stabbed him forty-seven times, leaving him dead. Four years later Mxenge's widow, Victoria, was shot and hacked to death in front of her children in the driveway of her home in Umlazi.

Soon after the killing, Coetzee suggested to Colonel Nick van Rensberg, the head of the security police in Port Elizabeth, that he could assist him in solving "a problem" that van Rensburg was faced with. The 'problem' took the form of a man named Sizwe Kondile. The security police had detained him after he had been arrested entering South Africa with false papers. In the subsequent interrogation and torture, he sustained injuries to his head. Concerned that they might have another Biko situation on their hands, van Rensburg told Coetzee that Kondile would have to be killed. Coetzee suggested bringing the prisoner to Komatipoort. Coetzee had procured knockout drops from General Lothar Neethling and then spiked a drink that he gave to Kondile.

Victoria Mxenge, shot down in her driveway four years after Vlakplaas operatives had murdered her husband. (*In the Heart of the Whore* by Jacques Pauw, published by Southern Book Publishers)

After Kondile had passed out and was lying unconscious on the ground, one of the policeman shot him in the back of the head with a Makarov pistol. A pyre was built out of wood and car tyres and the body put on the pyre to burn. Beers were opened and while the corpse burned, the policemen barbequed their steak, chops and *boerewors* (farm sausage) on a fire next to the pyre.[2]

During an operation in Swaziland Coetzee and his men were told to scout out suitable ANC targets and to blow them up. After a few days, as nothing had happened, Brigadier Willem Schoon summoned Coetzee back to Pretoria to explain his inaction. While Coetzee was absent the askaris in Swaziland stumbled on Joe Pillay who was suspected of being an ANC member. They grabbed Pillay, who struggled, screamed and fought back, making so much noise that he attracted the attention of some members of the public. One of the onlookers took down the registration number of the car he was being forced into and reported what he had seen to the Swazi police. The unsuspecting askaris dropped Pillay at the Swazi border with South Africa and, after being detained overnight, policeman from Ermelo brought Pillay to Vlakplaas. The askaris returned to Swaziland to carry out more 'hits', unaware that the abduction of Pillay had been reported. On their reentry into Swaziland, the police identified the car, gave chase and arrested the askaris. Released on bail, they were smuggled across the border back into the safety of South Africa. Meanwhile, at Vlakplaas, Pillay was being beaten and interrogated, but it soon became apparent that he was not involved with the ANC at all. But the damage had been done. Swazi officials, aware of the abduction demanded his release and an apology from the South African Security Branch. General Johann Coetzee assured the Swazi delegates that Dirk Coetzee and his men had acted as a rogue unit without official sanction, and offered his apologies. Brigadier Schoon was furious with Coetzee for the mix-up, and it was probably this event more than any other that led to Coetzee's rapid fall from grace in the South African Police force.[3]

In 1981 Coetzee was involved in a number of murders apart from that of Griffiths Mxengu. All were as identified ANC activists such as the Lesotho-based Vuyani Mavuso and Peter Dlamini who were taken by Coetzee and Major Koos Vemeulen to a spot near Komatipoort. Here they were given knockout drops that didn't work before being shot anyway by Vermeulen. Their bodies were again burned on a pyre while Coetzee, Vermeulen and the askaris cracked open a few beers and enjoyed a *braai*. Moema was another ANC activist murdered by Coetzee.[4]

In Coetzee's operations the line between the law and the underworld became very blurred. Making money illegally from the sale of a victim's possessions, drug-dealing, illicit diamond-dealing and pornography all became part of Coetzee's brief.

In December 1981, after Coetzee had embarrassed his superiors in the security police just once too often, he was removed from Vlakplaas. By this time there were seventeen askaris serving on the farm.[5] In January 1982, he was transferred to police headquarters in Pretoria. This move heralded his fall from grace and one lowly posting was followed by another until he ended up where his career had begun, back in the Flying Squad. He was succeeded by Jack Cronjé until Eugene de Kock was appointed Vlakplaas commander in 1985

Known by a variety of nicknames—'Brille' (spectacles: he wore thick 'milk-bottle-bottom-type' spectacles), 'Prime Evil' or 'Fok Fok de Kock'—he had grown up in an ordinary Afrikaans family in Pretoria. His father was a magistrate and a member of the extreme right-wing secret organization Die Broederbond (The Brotherhood) reserved exclusively for 'pure Afrikaners'.

After completing high school, de Kock attempted to join the army and applied for a commission. He was rejected because of his stuttering. He then joined the South African Police and, like his colleague Coetzee, received his training at the South African Police College in 1976, one year after Dirk Coetzee had completed his. One of de Kock's colleagues at police training college said, "We were taught to hate. For five weeks we were subjected to the ranting and raving of a lecturer who was a cross between Eugene Terre'Blanche [leader of the Afrikaner Weerstandsbeweging, the

Vlakplaas commander, Eugene de Kock.

AWB, an extreme right-wing group] and Hitler. We were told that black people were less civilized than white people and were unable to differentiate between right and wrong. People worked us up into fervor."

While at police training college, de Kock applied to join the Special Task Force. He was rejected, this time because of his poor eyesight. After police training de Kock was sent as a member of the SAP to assist the Rhodesians in the fight against Nkomo's and Mugabe's guerrilla forces. It was in Rhodesia that he learned his techniques and earned the reputation of being a ruthless and efficient killing machine. He served ten tours of three months each there. After Rhodesia, de Kock went on to fight in Ovamboland, South West Africa, against SWAPO. He was a founder member of Koevoet, the special police unit that was feared by locals and SWAPO alike. Craig Williamson, later known as South Africa's 'Superspy' and even later a member of parliament, described de Kock as "fearless. He was a leader who led from the front and by example. He was nicknamed 'the Lion'." In one 'contact' alone in Ovamboland, de Kock and his men of Section ZD killed twenty-seven of the enemy.

*Above and facing top*: Counterinsurgency operations in Rhodesia.

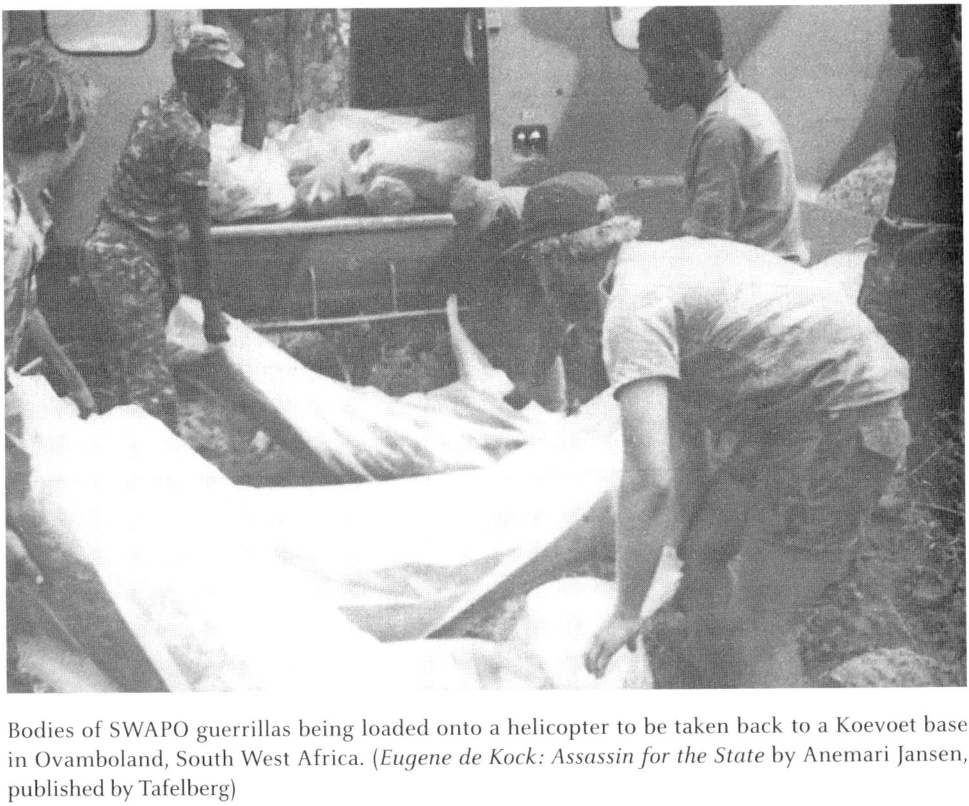

Bodies of SWAPO guerrillas being loaded onto a helicopter to be taken back to a Koevoet base in Ovamboland, South West Africa. (*Eugene de Kock: Assassin for the State* by Anemari Jansen, published by Tafelberg)

The South African government paid a bounty of R2,000 per head (at the time around £1,200) for those killed. De Kock adapted Mao's philosophy on insurgency and used it against the insurgents themselves. When interrogating a captured cadre, de Kock would cut off his prisoner's ears. One of his colleagues who served with de Kock described him: "He was a hard man ... he was a soldier. Killing was his job. He felt nothing for his victims. He was cold-blooded terror."

In 1982 de Kock was a member of an eight-man team sent to London on the orders of P. W. Botha, the president, to plant a bomb at the offices of the ANC in London. The order to carry out the bombing was given to the head of the security police, Johann Coetzee, by the minister of law and order Louis le Grange. De Kock at the time was serving in Ovamboland with Koevoet. He was approached by Craig Williamson of the National Intelligence Service (NIS) to join the team to carry out the bombing. The eleven kilograms of explosives required for the bomb were sent to a South African operative in London, Peter Casselton, in a diplomatic bag. Another NIS agent assembled the bomb in London. De Kock and John Adam were then equipped for the operation by being provided with false passports, travellers' cheques and clothes.

On arrival in London they spent time across the road from the ANC offices in a pub, studying the target. Meanwhile, two of the agents, Roger Raven and Peter Casselton, had a lucky escape. After assembling the bomb, the pair was driving across London in a hired car with the bomb on the back seat when a policewomen stopped them on a routine security check (it was the time of the IRA's mainland bombing campaign). She asked Casselton the registration number of the car they were driving. Fortunately for them he remembered it and they were waved through without further ado.

On the 14 March 1982, an hour before midnight, the group of eight climbed over the back gate of the ANC premises. As they huddled together in the dark, someone asked the question, "Where's the bomb?" There was a moment's silence. It had been left, forgotten, on the other side of the wall. It had to be retrieved. So after climbing back over the gate and retrieving it, it was placed at the back of the building next to a disused armchair. It exploded sometime later, causing extensive damage to the offices and injuring an ANC security guard who was asleep upstairs at the time. On his return to South Africa, de Kock was awarded the Police Star for Outstanding Service by Louis le Grange.[6]

The London operation to blow up the ANC offices was not the only sabotage attack authorized by President P. W. Botha. There were at least two other sabotage attacks that he personally authorized, both in South Africa. These were state-sanctioned acts of terrorism. Botha was later to be found guilty of contempt of court when he refused to comply with a summons to appear before the Truth and Reconciliation Commission to answer these and other charges.

After the bombing of the ANC offices in London.

As mentioned, Vlakplaas was awash with drugs, sex and booze. As such it was a highly attractive destination for visiting generals and ministers who would fly in from Pretoria, landing on the helipad built specially to facilitate their visits. The white policemen attached to Vlakplaas spent their mornings doing their 'admin', filling in fictitious expense claims both for their own personal enrichment as well as funding their operations. All of the parties—and there were plenty—thrown at Vlakplaas for the pleasure of the generals were paid for by fictitious expense claims. Between fifty and hundred people attended theses parties and alcohol flowed freely. So extensive were the claims that de Kock had three or four of his men filling in fictitious claims sometimes for a week at a time. These claims bought ice machines, pool tables, booze and women.[7] Hundreds of thousands of rands were embezzled from state coffers in this manner. Sometimes individual claims amounted to R80,000 (approximately £50,000 at the time) or more. Alcohol flowed freely. The more than forty askaris fought among themselves and smoked *dagga*. The white operatives fiddled expenses and partied. And partied. And partied. Some afternoons, strippers from the Polaris Hotel in Erasmia were fetched and brought to Vlakplaas, along with further cases and cases of booze. The strippers performed under the gazebo in the entertainment area while de Kock sat in the snooker room, brooding.

The golden days of the Polaris Hotel have long since faded. (Robin Binckes)

Vlakplaas adopted the emblem of the honey badger. Their motto was 'Invisible. Invincible'. They chose the honey badger as it is recorded in the *Guinness Book of Records* as the world's most fearless creature. It will attack any enemy including man. Their jaws are so powerful that they are able to crunch through the shell of a tortoise and will attack any animal including lion and leopard without fear.

Visitors to Vlakplaas were traditionally given a drink called '*leeu tande*' (lion's teeth) as an initiation drink. Made from crushed garlic and a mixture of every type of alcohol available at the time, visitors were forced to drink the potion. So foul was the taste that frequently the visitors vomited the contents onto the ground. Those who refused to drink '*leeu tande*' had their neckties cut off.

Discipline among the askaris at Vlakplaas was always a problem. While it was accepted that they efficiently carried out operations against ANC and PAC activists, they were never really trusted by their white colleagues. The askaris had changed sides once, which meant they could do it again. One of the askaris murdered because of this sentiment was Pumelelo Moses Nthelang, known as 'Geletjie'.

In June 1989 de Kock and a group of Vlakplaas operatives were travelling back from an aborted operation near the Swazi border. The men stopped at various bars on the way, drank heavily and bought more beers for the journey. When they arrived back at Vlakplaas de Kock opened the canteen and they carried on drinking, playing billiards in the snooker room.

Willie Nortje, de Kock's long-time friend and comrade, talking to Koevoet members at Oshakati, Ovamboland, in the early 1980s.

A white operator, Bellinghan, approached de Kock, "That bastard Nthelang is back."

Nthelang had not reported for duty for some days and de Kock suspected that he might be a double agent secretly working for the ANC. "Where is he?" asked de Kock.

"He's here. We found him in a shebeen [unlicensed tavern] in Laudium. He's very drunk".

"Bring him here," de Kock commanded.

A few minutes later a surly, drunk Nthelang was brought before de Kock. "Where the hell have you been and what have you been up to?" asked de Kock.

Nthelang didn't answer the question but instead informed de Kock that his service pistol was missing and that it had been stolen from him at the shebeen.

De Kock flew into a rage and picked up a snooker cue and lashed Nthelang over the head with the heavier end. He struck him three more times over the head and would have continued had the cue not snapped with the force of the blows. He then struck Nthelang on the side of the head with his fist. Nthelang fell to the floor. De Kock stormed out of the canteen, his face flushed with anger and went to his office to regain his composure. Meanwhile, as Nthelang lay senseless on the ground, a number of the drunk white operatives began to kick and beat him in an attempt to get him to tell them what had happened to his weapon. Finally he was 'tubed', a common practice at Vlakplaas. The inner tube of a car tyre was cut into sections. One section was

The *braai* area at Vlakplaas situated next to the snooker room. (Robin Binckes)

then placed over Nthelang's head and face making it very difficult to breathe. At the same time he was hit and kicked by a number of the men.

There was a moment of quiet when someone called out in the middle of the beating. "He's not breathing. He's dead."

Nthelang lay still on the floor of the entertainment area. Bellinghan hurried to de Kock's office and informed him as to what had happened.

"Now there'll be a big problem," said de Kock. "We have to find a way to get rid of the body. Quickly, get a blanket and fold up the body. Contact Ras. He must find us a place where we can bury it. Get rid of all the blood and clean up the canteen. Nobody must know about this."

Ras arrived and the blanketed body was put into the boot of the car and Ras, de Kock, Snyders, Flores and Willemse drove to a farm in the Western Transvaal (now North West province) where they went about preparing a grave. The farm owner, who was well known to Ras, was not informed of the digging or its purpose, but when he saw five burly policemen with shovels he must have guessed what the mission was about. They carried the now-stiff corpse from the car after digging the shallow grave and they piled rubbish and boxes on top of the body. Discussion was held as to whether or not the body should be burned. It was decided not and the hole was filled in.

Vlakplaas operative Riaan Bellinghan ('Balletjies') during an askari training session. (*Eugene de Kock: Assassin for the State* by Anemari Jansen, published by Tafelberg)

Large-calibre bullet holes in a steel fencing standard at Vlakplaas. (Robin Binckes)

On return to Vlakplaas, de Kock instructed Baker to open a file for a missing person. To cover up the murder, he arranged that Nthelang's mother would receive Nthelang's salary payments for the next six months as a missing person.

In 2014, de Kock was allowed out of prison to work with Madeleine Fullard and the Missing Persons Task Team, and, accompanied by Ras, they finally located Nthelang.'s grave. [8]Nthelang was twenty-two years old when he was murdered.

Japie Maponya's disappearance was a direct result of cooperation between Vlakplaas and the Krugersdorp security police. Oderile Maponya was a member of the ANC and MK. The Krugersdorp Security Police were searching for him. In an effort to track him down the Krugersdorp police had questioned his brother Japie on a number of occasions as to his brother's whereabouts but he claimed he knew nothing. The police did not believe him. Eugene de Kock was called in. He arrived at Krugersdorp and was introduced to General Johann le Roux. Le Roux asked de Kock to assist and to abduct Japie Maponya and interrogate him to find out where his brother Oderile was hiding. De Kock agreed and asked le Roux what he wanted done with Maponya after they had finished interrogating him. Le Roux replied, "I never want to see him again in Krugersdorp." De Kock was happy to oblige.

One evening three askaris waited outside the Krugersdorp bank where he worked. As he came out of the building he was grabbed and bundled into a waiting vehicle and driven to Vlakplaas.

He was taken down to the one *braai* area on the banks of the Hennops river. It was here that the operatives would frequently party and relax, swimming in the river or playing on the '*foefie*' slide, the zip slide. He was beaten and questioned by de Kock. He was then 'tubed' and given the helicopter treatment, this time suspended from a tree before being thrown into a locked minibus and sprayed with teargas. But Maponya refused to talk, very possibly because he did not know where his brother was. De Kock then decided that Maponya had to be permanently removed as he had now witnessed Vlakplaas in all its gory detail. Accompanied by Eugene Fourie, Willie Nortje and David van der Walt, de Kock drove with the badly beaten Maponya to Piet Retief near the Swazi border. They stopped at the home of Warrant Officer Freek Pienaar and collected a pick, spade and garden fork from him. They then drove toward the border at Nerston and travelled to a secluded, forested spot on the border two or three kilometres away from the border post. De Kock and Nortje then climbed through border fence dragging the handcuffed Maponya with them. After walking some eighty metres into the forest, Nortje smashed Maponya over the head with the butt of his Uzi submachine gun. Maponya fell to the ground unconscious. The blow had caused the Uzi to jam. De Kock attempted to clear the jam but was unsuccessful so he went back to the car and returned with a subsonic 9mm cartridge which Nortje loaded into his pistol. By this time, Maponya had recovered consciousness and, realizing what was happening, with hands handcuffed behind his back, attempted to flee. De Kock hit him over the head with a spade and grabbed him, holding him while he struggled to break free. Nortje then shot him in the temple, killing him instantly.[9] They buried him in a shallow grave.

As activism against the apartheid government burgeoned in the 1980s, regional security branches such as the Eastern Cape and other killing units were no less violent and brutal than Vlakplaas. One of the most affected areas was the Eastern Cape, always a hotbed of resistance. So turbulent was the area that in May 1985 President Botha, defence minister Malan and deputy minister of defence Adrian Vlok visited the region and instructed the local security forces that the area "had to be stabilized at all costs". To the Eastern Cape security police "at all costs" meant the elimination of identified troublemakers. Gideon Niewoudt, the man who had beaten Steve Biko to death, took charge. He was known in the Eastern Cape as the 'Angel of Death'.

Sipho Hashe, Champion Galela and Qaqawuli Godolozi were members of the Port Elizabeth Black Civic Organization (PEBCO). The three were known to the security branch as the PEBCO Three. Posing as an activist, one of Niewoudt's men set up a meeting with the three. When the three arrived at the meeting place they were seized

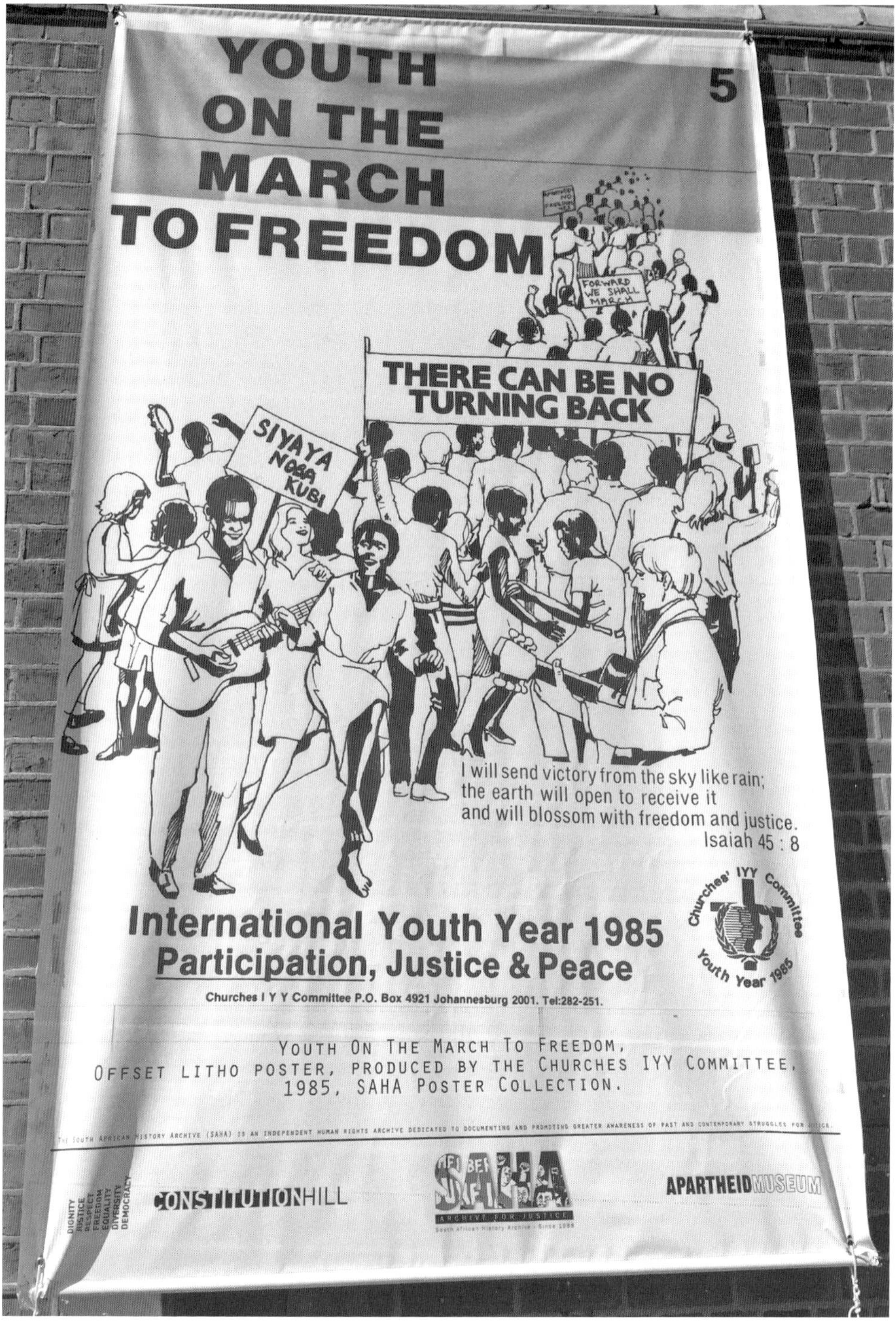


Youth on the March to Freedom banner. (Robin Binckes)

*Above left*: Gideon Niewoudt of the Eastern Cape security police, known as the 'Angel of Death', seen here at the TRC hearings. (*Apartheid's Friends* by James Sanders, published by John Murray Press, an imprint of Hodder & Stoughton)

*Above right*: Reverend Frank Chicane, one of Vlok's intended victims. (*In the Heart of the Whore* by Jacques Pauw, published by Southern Book Publishers)

and taken to an isolated police station at Post Chalmers near Cradock. According to evidence of askaris at the TRC hearings, Niewoudt and his security police interrogated Galela and tortured him to death. With Galela's body in full view, Hashe was then subjected to the same torture until he too died. Godolozi was left all night with the two bodies of his colleagues before he too was murdered the next day. Their bodies were thrown into the Fish River.

Six weeks later, still in the Eastern Cape, Mathew Goniwe, Sparrow Mkhonto, Fort Calata and Sicelo Mhlawuli, known as the Cradock Four, were murdered. The four had been watched by the security police and like the PEBCO Three identified as troublemakers. Brigadier Joffel van der Westhuizen, military commander of the Eastern Cape, issued a signal recommending that "Goniwe and Calata as a matter of urgency be permanently removed from society".

The State Security Council had discussed Goniwe's 'removal' a year before his death. The meeting was attended by P. W. Botha, Pik Botha, F. W. de Klerk and Barend du Plessis, the minister for black education. Du Plessis told the meeting that there were two ex-teachers in the Eastern Cape who were political agitators. "It would be good if they could be removed," he told the meeting. Removed they were. Eugene de Kock was called in to assist. On the night of 27 June 1985 Captain Johann van Zyl led a team comprised of Lieutenant Eric Taylor, Sergeant Gerhardus Lotz and three black security policemen that intercepted Goniwe's car as it headed toward Cradock on the way back from Port Elizabeth where the four had attended a meeting. The four men were handcuffed and then driven to a remote area. Colonel van Rensburg had briefed the police beforehand. "Make it look like a vigilante or AZAPO attack." The four men were stabbed to death. Then the handcuffs were removed, petrol poured over the bodies which together with the car were then set alight.

In early December 1987 the Northern Transvaal (now Limpopo province) Security Branch operatives killed one of their own police colleagues with an exemplary police record because it was believed he was providing sensitive information to the ANC in Zimbabwe. Philipus Loots, who was a captain in the security police, was called to the office of Colonel Ras, together with Captain Hechter and Captain van Vuuren. Ras informed them that he had been told by Brigadier Stemmet that the policeman, Richard Motasi, based in Hammanskraal north of Pretoria, was an ANC agent and had to be eliminated. Joe Mamasela was tasked with confirming Motasi's address and establishing what car he would be driving. Mamasela confirmed the information that afternoon.

That same night, 1 December 1987, the death squad left to carry out their instructions. In a car driven by Danny Selahle, Joe Mamasela, Loots, Hechter and van Vuuren set off for Hammanskraal. They arrived at Motasi's address and saw that a light was on in the front room of the house, the living room. Mamasela knocked on the door, which was opened by Richard's wife Irene Motasi who informed Mamasela that her husband had not yet returned from work. Mamasela reported back to the men in the car. After a brief discussion they sent Mamasela back to the house. Mamasela knocked on the door again. When Irene opened the door, watched by her five-year-old son Tsidiso, Mamasela grabbed the woman and forcibly dragged her to the bedroom. He then dragged the screaming five-year-old into the same bedroom and locked the door. Hechter, van Vuuren and Loots then entered the house and sat in the living room to await the arrival of their target, Richard Motasi. Mamasela remained in the bedroom guarding Irene Motasi and her son. The men in the living room made sure that the curtains were fully closed and left the television on so that the unsuspecting Motasi would see the flickering of the television on his arrival which would provide an air of normality. After waiting a short while the four men heard the sound of a car pulling up outside; the car door slammed followed by the sound of footsteps as Motasi approached the front door. As he opened the door, Hechter grabbed Motasi who immediately lashed out at him in fright. Hechter struggled to overpower Motasi who fought like a wild animal realizing that his life was in danger. Loots attempted to assist Hechter and swung the back of his pistol toward Motasi's head. He struck Hechter by mistake. Despite the blow Hechter began to get the better of Motasi. He grabbed a cushion from one of the living room chairs and held it over the struggling Motasi's face. Van Vuuren then fired four shots from an AK-47 into Motasi's head. The pillow served to muffle the sound. They left the body on the floor.

Hechter ordered van Vuuren to call Mamasela from the bedroom. "Let's get out of here," he said.

Van Vuuren went to the bedroom and shouted through the door, "Come on. It's over. Let's go."

Mamasela unlocked the door and looked back at the bed where a terrified Irene Motasi lay sobbing. Realizing that she could identify him, he strode to the bedside, grabbed a pillow, covered her head with it and fired several shots at point-blank range into her head while the hysterical boy Tsidiso looked on. The men hurried out of the house and joined Danny Sehlale in the car. As they drove off into the night the light from the television flickered cheerfully.

The next morning Richard Motasi's mother-in-law, Gloria Hlabangane, worried that she hadn't heard from her daughter, went to the house. The door was open. The living room was a mess from the struggle the night before. Chairs and side tables were overturned. The television was still on. On the floor lay the body of Richard. He had been shot in the ear and pieces of his skull and brains lay on the floor. Her instincts kicked in. What about Tsidiso? Where was her grandson? In a panic she ran from the living room to Tsidiso's bedroom leaving the body of her son-in-law lying in the congealed blood. The room was a complete mess. Police trunks containing documents had been tipped over and papers were scattered across the room. There was no sign of the little boy. She worried in case his body lay under the pile of papers. Suddenly she heard a sound behind her. She turned. The boy stood trembling, looking at her. He had spent the whole night, alone, with the bodies of his parents.

"*Gogo baba bulayile,*" (Granny they have killed him) he said, sobbing.

"*Ngubane?*" (Who?)

"*Amaphoyisa,*" (the police) he answered

"*Wazi kanyani?*" (How do you know?)

"*Keba bone with kadi jerseys ne ba apere dijersey tse tswanang letsa papa waka.*" (They were wearing jerseys that look like my father's.)[10]

# 4. CIVIL COOPERATION BUREAU

The Civil Cooperation Bureau (CCB) was established by the Special Forces in 1986. The CCB was comprised of operatives who were mainly military, drawn from ex-Recce and ex-Koevoet members, and which was liberally laced with known criminals and killers.

The long-term goal of the CCB was to create a global network of companies that would both be legitimate businesses as well as fronts for South Africa's operations directed at enemies of apartheid. Headed by businessmen their function would be to run the companies successfully while at the same time collecting intelligence and, when asked, to act on it. This was referred to as their 'blue-line cover'—a respectable business providing cover for shady operations. Top military personnel were identified to join the CCB. These had to immediately resign their commissions in the SADF. Despite having no connection with the military, the CCB was still able to call on specialized SADF units such as SAMS (South African Medical Services) for chemical and biological warfare and the EMLC (Electronic Magnetic Logistical Component) for specialized weapons such as briefcase bombs, letter bombs and explosive devices. Joe Verster, head of the CCB, assumed the *noms de guerre* of Rick van Staden and Dave Martin for his operations.

Initially the CCB operated outside the borders of South Africa but an internal component was added in 1988. Structured like a company along regional lines, there were eight geographical regions and two organizational divisions, Intelligence & Finance, and Administration. The chairman of the board was initially Major-General 'Joep' Joubert but Major-General Eddie Webb replaced him in 1989. The managing director was Joe Verster and his deputy was Dawid Fourie. Board members included Wouter Basson (later to become known as 'Dr Death'), Theuns Kruger and Lafras Luitingh. Others in the inner circle included Christoffel Nel and commandants Charl Naudé and Corrie Meerholtz.

Within the CCB there were two types of member: the 'aware' and the 'unaware'. The 'awares' were recruited from the ranks of the SADF who would then employ staff, the 'unawares'. The 'awares' would set up blue-line operations that the 'unawares' executed, in most instances completely oblivious that they were working for a state security organization. They all signed contracts with 'The Organization' and worked from Special Forces headquarters known as '*Die Gat*' (The Hole). Some 'unawares' knew it was a government department that they worked for but were not too sure what part of government. Verster estimated that there were about 150 'aware' members and a hundred 'unaware' employees. In addition the CCB employed local and international

## Project Coast

Wouter Basson, a qualified medical doctor and specialist physician, joined the SADF in 1975. Six years later he was promoted to lieutenant-colonel and was ordered by the Surgeon General to establish a chemical and biological warfare (CBW) capability, Project Coast, with an annual budget of more than $10 million to develop chemical and biological agents. A front company, Delta G Scientific, was set up, employing more than 200 staff working on the development of chemical agents in three categories: lethal, incapacitating and irritating.[1] Another front company, Roodeplaat Research Laboratories, tested the biological effects of various toxins.

Basson was given 200,000 mandrax tablets that had been confiscated by the drug squad, as well as LSD and marijuana In 1988 Delta G Scientific produced a tonne of the sedative methaqualone (mandrax) as well as a tonne of ecstasy. Basson travelled extensively, building a network of contacts in the shady world of CBW. He visited Croatia, Taiwan, the U.S., West Germany and Israel.[2]

Some of the more infamous cases included 200 SWAPO prisoners who were injected with muscle-relaxants and incapacitated before being flown out to sea and thrown out the aircraft.[3] Reverend Frank Chikane, a high-profile anti-apartheid leader, fell ill in South West Africa in 1989. He was flown to Johannesburg for treatment and diagnosed with 'acute gastroenteritis'. After four days in hospital, he was discharged but on a visit to the United States a few days later he again became ill and was admitted to hospital. Again he recovered but after his fourth collapse and hospital stay, doctors diagnosed organophosphate poisoning. It is believed that CCB agents had contaminated his baggage or clothing with toxins. In 1992 chemicals were used against Frelimo troops in an operation near the Mozambican border. Some died and others had to be hospitalized.[4]

Many Project Coast plans never reached fruition, some being bizarrely James Bondish: a plot to assassinate prominent ANC figures Ronnie Kasrils and Pallo Jordan in London using the tip of an umbrella laced with deadly poison (a technique perfected by the KGB), distributing poisoned cans of beer, developing sterility drugs to be used in water reservoirs supplying black townships in order to reduce the black birth rate, lacing cigarettes with anthrax spores and chocolate with cyanide, development of a drug to change white people into black for a short time to allow them to infiltrate the ranks of the ANC and manufacturing mortar bombs filled with methaqualone to pacify rioting crowds.

When Dr Basson was arrested in 1997 he had in his possession 1,000 ecstasy capsules. He appeared to be about to carry off his own drug deal.[5]

criminals to carry out their dirty work both locally and internationally. 'Peaches' Gordon, Donald Acheson and Isgak Hardien were three of those who fell into this category. Some of the main characters of Region Six who were assigned to various subregions were Abram 'Slang' (Snake) van Zyl in the Western Cape, 'Chappies' Maree in Natal and 'Calla' Botha in the Transvaal (now Gauteng province). Ferdi Barnard was also a member of Region Six.

The objective of the CCB was "the maximal disruption of the enemy". Again, the enemy was perceived to be the communists and, by association, the ANC, the PAC and any other 'liberation' movement. The CCB prescribed maximum disruption to be achieved by one or all of the following methods: death, infiltration, bribery, compromise or blackmail and destruction.[6]

David Webster, shot by Ferdi Barnard in a drive-by shooting as he was unloading plants from his car. (*In the Heart of the Whore* by Jacques Pauw, published by Southern Book Publishers)

One of their targets was a young anthropologist with high ideals. David Webster was an avid fan of the Soweto-based soccer team Kaiser Chiefs. After working in Mozambique, on his return to South Africa he became acutely aware of the injustices in the country and became a human rights activist. He was low profile and did not seek recognition or reward. He played an important role in the founding of the Detainees Parents Support Committee and played an active role in providing support to political detainees and their families. In 1989 he wrote a report for the Human Rights Commission about the activities of the South African government and their oppressive system, quoting examples of torture, abduction and murder. These claims did little to endear him to the security organs of the state, particularly the CCB.

On the evening of 1 May 1989, Webster and his partner of some years, Maggie Friedman, were returning to their house in Troyeville, Johannesburg. Webster was busy offloading from his pick-up truck plants which he and Maggie had purchased for their garden from a nursery. Three members of the CCB were watching: Ferdie Barnard was wearing a blond wig as disguise and was sitting in the back of the car driven by Eugene Riley, with Calla Botha in the front passenger seat. Barnard recognized the moment as perfect for carrying out the assassination. He ordered Riley to drive past Webster and Friedman. Barnard then opened fired at close range. Webster was hit in the chest. Maggie Friedman screamed. Later she recalled, "I heard a sound like a car backfiring and David fell and clutched his chest and called out, 'Call an ambulance. I've been shot by a shotgun.'" He died thirty minutes later.

Despite suspicions that the assassination had been carried out by the CCB and despite the arrest of Ferdi Barnard, nothing could be proved and Barnard was soon released. Barnard, however, could not keep quiet and had bragged about the murder to Kevin Trytsman while under arrest. Later he was to confess to his wife of the time, Maryna Language, and later still to investigative journalist, Jacques Pauw. He told Pauw that he had shot Webster and described what had happened: "He flew through the air and landed on the pavement."

Maryna Language testified to the TRC that the CCB supplied Ferdie Barnard with a list of people to eliminate that included ANC Women's League President Winnie Mandela, Archbishop Desmond Tutu, SWAPO activist Anton Lubowski, SA Communist Party leader Chris Hani and David Webster. Until Webster was killed Maryna Language did not believe Barnard's wild claims of killing and believed that Barnard lived in a dreamworld.

Barnard was paid R40,000 (around £25,000) for carrying out this assignment. (Maryna Language testified that the amount paid to him was R90,000 (around £53,000) which he used as a deposit on a new house.) In 1998, Ferdi Barnard was sentenced to life imprisonment for Webster's murder.

Ferdi Barnard who assassinated David Webster. (*Dances With Devils* by Jacques Pauw, published by Zebra Press, an imprint of Struik Publishers)

Anti-apartheid poster. (Robin Binckes)

Mozambique provided refuge to a number of ANC activists and insurgents. Two of these were Albie Sachs (now a retired Constitutional Court judge) and Indres Naidoo who both lived and worked in Maputo. Albie Sachs's work at that time was working for the Mozambican Ministry of Justice dealing in family law and court structures. At the same time he travelled to and from Lusaka to consult with Oliver Tambo, head of the ANC in exile, on the formulation of a new South African constitution for the day when the ANC came to power. Sachs and Naidoo were kept under surveillance by the CCB and were both 'profiled' by Henri van der Westhuizen as targets. Naidoo was recognized as an ANC activist who played a key role in secretly infiltrating

ANC members across the border into Natal and the Eastern Transvaal (now KwaZulu-Natal and Mpumulanga provinces).

At the end of March 1988, Albie Sachs, who had been a member of the Communist Party in South Africa, was attending an ANC workshop in Lusaka, Zambia, on Oliver Tambo's vision for a South African Bill of Rights under ANC control.

Former Constitutional Court judge Albie Sachs who lost an arm and an eye in a car bomb attack in Maputo. (Robin Binckes)

On 7 April, 1988 the high-profile ANC activist and champion of human rights walked to his car parked in a carpark near his Maputo apartment that was on the third floor of an apartment block on the corner of Julius Nyerere and Eduardo Mondlane streets. As he opened the door on the driver's side, there was a massive explosion as the bomb planted by a CCB operative detonated. Sachs was thrown to the ground by the blast. Pieces of metal from the twisted wreckage of the car landed nine floors up. Sachs was severely injured and was nearly killed: his right arm was torn from his body and left hanging from shreds of skin (it was subsequently amputated) and he was blinded in his right eye. Two innocent Mozambicans walking past at the critical moment were hit by the blast and died after being taken to hospital. The car was a left-hand drive red Honda. Left-hand drive cars are unusual in Mozambique as, like South Africa, driving is on the left-hand side of the road so most cars are right-hand drive. It was this that saved Sachs's life, so he believes, as the bomb was planted under the right-hand side of the Honda.

Pieter Botes, a senior member of the CCB, told Jacues Pauw that he had planned the attack on Albie Sachs and that he had arranged for the bomb to be made by Colonel Hekkies van Heerden[7] and then delivered. He had then appointed a black member of the CCB to plant the bomb. The man who planted the bomb was rewarded by the CCB with R4,000 (around £2,500) after the operation. In his application for amnesty before the Truth and Reconciliation Commission in 2000 Henri van der Westhuizen stated that Albie Sachs was not the target that day and that the bomb was intended to kill Indres Naidoo. Van der Westhuizen's job at CCB was to prepare files containing details of prominent ANC activists in Maputo who had been identified as possible assassination targets by TREWITS (Counter-Revolutionary Information Target Centre established in 1985 by the security forces to identify possible targets).

Van der Westhuizen had handed over the file identifying Naidoo as the target to Pieter Botes. Naidoo was supposed to be using the car that day but Albie Sachs had opened the car door and took the full blast of the explosion. Van der Westhuizen claimed that Pieter Botes had replaced Albie Sachs as the target. Sachs disagrees with van der Westhuizen: "It was my car and although I lent it to Indres when I was away there was no reason why he would have been driving the car that day."[8] As Sachs was wheeled to the aircraft that was to fly him out of Mozambique to safety, he remembers saying to himself, "No more guns. No more guns"[9]

In 1998 van der Westhuizen was granted an appointment to see Judge Albie Sachs in his chambers to apologize for the role he played in nearly killing him. Sachs described the visit in a written statement he made to the Truth and Reconciliation Commission. Here is the transcript of that statement which was read out in court:

> Amnesty Application by Mr Henri van der Westhuizen—Statement by Albie Sachs
>
> I was in my chambers about two years ago when I received a message from reception that somebody calling himself Henri had arrived to see me. I went to the security entrance with a measure of anticipation. Henri had telephoned a few days earlier to say that he was going to testify to the Truth and Reconciliation Commission about the bomb which had led to my car exploding and I losing my right arm. Naturally I was keen to see the person who had the courage or the foolhardiness or just the interest, to want to see me.
>
> I opened the door with my security pass and a slender youngish man came forward. He introduced himself as Henri and gave the surname. Who was this person whom I had never seen until that moment? Who did not know me, who had no anger towards me, whom I did not hate, for whom I was just a figure? Who had tried to extinguish my life? What passed through his head, how had he functioned, how did he fit into the group that was on the other side [the enemy, the apartheid state], which was almost as anonymous to me as I was to them? I did not wish to pre-empt the interrogation of the Commission. I just wanted him to say as much as he was willing to say.
>
> He would have seen the dossier on me, it would have shown that I had been in exile in Mozambique, neighbouring South Africa, working on the reconstruction of the Mozambique legal system. That although I had been an active member of the African National Congress and especially on the Constitutional Committee, I was not involved in any underground activity or military or intelligence work at all. Yet they had chosen me and tried to eliminate me. Why? I was an intellectual and challenged their claim that no political system could be found to enable black and white to live together as equals in South Africa. Every intellectual dreams of being taken seriously by someone, but not that seriously.
>
> We spoke for about two hours. He looked at me almost with a measure of jealousy. Here he was, sitting in my chambers, beautiful pictures on the walls.

I was a Judge of the Constitutional Court, the highest court in the country, and he was now a demobilized soldier, with a torn past and a fragmented future. He had not even been given a golden handshake, but a brass one, a modest sum of money compared to what the retiring Generals had got. Yet he had been willing to invest his energies, his intelligence, maybe even his life, for his country, for apartheid and now he had been cast aside. He too had injuries, he told me; he had been shot in the leg and walked with a slight limp. He seemed petulant. I was on the court and he was unemployed. We would have gone on eyeing each other and talking forever. I stood up and said: "Henri a cheap emotion surged in me. I was tempted to say I cannot shake your hand, but you know why? Normally, if someone comes to my office, when I say goodbye I shake that person's hand, but I can't shake your hand. I can't now. Go to the Truth Commission, tell your story, help the country, do something for South Africa and then perhaps we can meet again."

When he walked back to the security door he was without the upright soldier's posture he had had before and looked uncomfortable, uneasy and sad. He went through the door. I said farewell, and he disappeared.

Some months later I was at a party in Johannesburg, feeling quite light-headed after a heavy year's work in court. In the midst of the music and hilarity, I heard a voice saying to me: "Hello." I turned around and saw a familiar face smiling at me, looking very happy. The person spoke again: "Hello, I am Henri, do you remember me?" He was beaming. I asked him what had happened. He told me that he had written to the TRC, giving them all the information he could and had applied for amnesty in relation to six different matters. Then he stopped talking, looked at me and said: "You told me that afterwards maybe" and I responded: "Yes, Henri, I said to you that afterwards, if you cooperated with the Truth Commission, if you did something for South Africa, maybe we could meet again. I've only got your word for it, but I can see from your face you are telling the truth." I put out my hand and shook his hand. He went away elated. I moved away and almost fainted in the arms of a friend of mine.

The Amnesty Committee is now hearing. I hope he is telling the truth and that he fulfils his side of the amnesty ... Sending him to jail won't make my arm come back, but living in an open and a democratic country has grown roses ... in the empty space. We've had too many bombs in this country, their bombs and our bombs. We need to solve our problems without violence. I wish Henri well. He had the courage to come and see me. We looked into one another's eyes and each found a person in the other. Now thanks to the orderly and humane process of the Truth Commission, we can live together in one country, not as predator and prey, but as equal citizens. That is my soft, irreplaceable joyous vengeance.[10]

# 5. SECURITY POLICE 'SUPERSPY'

The security police operated their own death squads. Key to their whole history is Craig Williamson, known in the media as 'Super Spy'. Williamson, an English-speaker with a private school education was an enigma. He joined the South African Police in 1968 and became a member of the security police in 1971. After successfully infiltrating various left-wing student organizations, he was elected to the Students' Representative Council of the University of Witwatersrand ('Wits') in 1973. His brief at university was to investigate the ANC and the South African Communist Party. During this time Williamson fed information back to the security police on subversive activities. He became so much part of the underground that during 1975/6 he was involved in assisting people who were on the run from the security police outside South Africa. Many of these exiles were being sent for training at one of the ANC bases outside South Africa. This helped establish his credibility. Nobody suspected that he could have been operating as an agent for the state. In 1975, while on the National Executive of the National Union of South African Students (NUSAS), he met and befriended a fellow member of the Executive, Jeanette Curtis who later married Marius Schoon. Williamson was later employed by NUSAS on a full-time basis and was perfectly positioned to carry out his spying role as his NUSAS job meant that he travelled to university campuses across the country to organize students on behalf of NUSAS.

As vice-president of NUSAS he travelled overseas fundraising until one of the overseas donors, the International University Exchange Fund (IUEF) snapped him up to work for them. He became the deputy director and in this position he diverted funds away from student bodies and student activities supporting the ANC. He siphoned off enough money to purchase a 'sister' farm to Vlakplaas, called Daisy and also situated outside Pretoria. This farm had far better facilities than Vlakplaas and in the modern, well-equipped classrooms and lecture halls, training programmes for security police were held. To balance his act, and his cover, Willliamson also arranged bursaries for black students. Although there were some who never fully trusted Williamson, the majority were taken in by his double act. After a fellow security policeman who had known Williamson since their days at Wits defected from the police and threatened to expose him, Williamson emerged from his double role, to work overtly as a major for the security police under Colonel Goosen.

Eugene de Kock later made a sworn statement that Craig Williamson was implicated in the assassination of Olof Palme, the Swedish prime minister, in 1986. This is

*Left*: Craig Williamson as a major in the South African Police, 1985. (Craig Williamson)

*Right*: Craig Williamson as the owner of Benson Craig (Pty) Ltd. In Botswana. (Craig Williamson)

denied by Williamson. However, the IUEF that Williamson infiltrated was a Swedish initiative run from Palme's office.[1] Williamson came to spend a great deal of time in Sweden getting to know not only the Swedish people but also the movements and habits of Olof Palme. In the 1980s Sweden led the way in imposing sanctions against South Africa and were major funders of the ANC. As such they became enemy number 1 in Operation Longreach, a dirty tricks operation funded by Military Intelligence and security police secret funds and headed up by Williamson who reported directly to the State Security Council (SSC). Longreach targeted apartheid's opponents in South Africa, Western Europe and the UK.

On 17 August 1982, Ruth First, the wife of activist Joe Slovo, was killed in Mozambique by a letter bomb sent by Williamson. Ruth First had met Joe Slovo in 1948 while Slovo was studying law. Both were members of the banned Communist Party. They married the following year. Ruth had travelled extensively, visiting Prague, Dubrovnik and Moscow for youth congresses and other conferences. Because of their communist sympathies both Joe and Ruth were arrested in 1956 on

Ruth First. (*In the Heart of the Whore* by Jacques Pauw, published by Southern Book Publishers)

charges of treason but the charges were dropped in 1958. Following the banning of the ANC after Sharpeville in 1960, Joe left South Africa in 1962 for exile in the United Kingdom. Ruth joined him there and played an active role in supporting the ANC, the Communist Party and the anti-apartheid movement. She taught at various universities in the UK before taking up the position of Director of Research at the Centre for African Studies at the Eduardo Mondlane University in Maputo, Mozambique, in 1978.

Williamson was given an official police envelope with a smaller envelope inside and instructions to meet with his direct superior, Brigadier Piet Goosen. On his arrival in Goosen's office, Goosen asked whether one of Williamsons 'technical operatives' could replace the documents in the smaller envelope with an explosive device that could kill one or both of the Slovos. Goosen explained that the smaller envelope had been intercepted by the security police and that after the device had been inserted, it would be sent on its way to the original addressee. Williamson carefully peered into the outer envelope and by using a pencil so as not to touch the documents saw that the envelope was addressed to someone at the Eduardo Mondlane University—Ruth First.

Williamson gave the task to Roger Raven who after a few days returned with the envelope. Williamson looked at the envelope and asked, "Would this device kill the two of us if it went off now?"

"Of course it would," Raven replied.

The envelope with the explosive device was then given to Goosen who arranged for the letter to be delivered to the university. Sometime later Ruth First was told by a colleague, Aquino de Bragança, at the university that there was a letter for her in the secretary's office. She collected the letter and returned to the room where her three colleagues—de Bragança, Pallo Jordan and Brgit O'Laughlin—were working. She opened the envelope. There was a massive explosion followed by two smaller explosions. The occupants of the room ducked as they thought they were under attack from outside. When the smoke cleared Ruth First lay dead on the floor, face-down, still wearing her white dress, red blazer and Italian shoes.

In 1977 Jeanette Curtis had married Marius Schoon. Jeanette had been extremely active in NUSAS and heavily involved with NUSWEL, the labour arm of NUSAS. She and Craig Williamson became close friends. She actively worked on mobilizing people into trade unions. Marius was a more high-profile activist and had already served twelve years' imprisonment for sabotage and at the time of their marriage he was still under house arrest with stringent orders restricting his freedom of movement and speech. Jeanette too had received banning orders for her trade union activities. On instructions from the ANC, the day after the two were married they illegally crossed the border into Botswana and claimed refugee status. Here they worked for the ANC mobilizing the masses back in South Africa. They recruited people in the PWV (Pretoria, Witwatersrand, Vaal) area of the Transvaal to send back reports about strategic events in their areas. Because of her extensive experience in working with unions Jeanette was also given the task of promoting the ANC to the powerful South African Congress of Trade Unions (COSATU). While in Botswana there were at least two failed attempts by security forces to assassinate Marius Schoon.

Prior to Williamson's 'coming out', he visited the Schoons in Botswana and stayed with them as a house guest on a number of occasions, using his friendship with Jeanette to gain access to their circle of friends and associates.

Both the Schoons worked for the International Voluntary Service (IVS) as field officers until their services were terminated after the Overseas Development Association, a British government organ, had informed the IVS that they considered the presence of the Schoons as a high risk to British volunteers in the IVS. After leaving the IVS in 1983, the Schoons were tipped off by the British high commissioner in Botswana that he had information that there was a conspiracy to kill Marius. The ANC redeployed the pair to Lusaka. In the short time they were in Zambia they felt threatened and frequently vacated their accommodation for fear of South African security force raids.

In December 1983, at the behest of the ANC, they moved to Lubango in Angola to teach English at the university there. At the time Lubango was on the front line of the conflict between the SADF and FAPLA (the Angolan army) and its Cuban allies. It was very much a military base with masses of FAPLA and Cuban soldiers and jeeps in the streets. Because of the strategic airport nearby the town came under aerial bombardment by the South African Air Force (SAAF) on several occasions.

Early in 1984, Brigadier Piet Goosen sent for Williamson and informed him that he had in his possession an intercepted letter from the ANC in Botswana to Marius and Jeanette Schoon in Angola. Goosen instructed Williamson to have a letter bomb made up by Williamson's star technician, Roger Raven. After completing the task, Raven gave the letter bomb to Willamson who handed it over to Brigadier Goosen. Knowing the destination of the letter bomb caused Williamson

*Above*: An SADF armoured battle group strikes into Angola.

*Left*: Jeannette Schoon, killed with her daughter by a letter bomb sent by Craig Williamson. (*In the Heart of the Whore* by Jacques Pauw, published by Southern Book Publishers)

some discomfort but, satisfying himself that the Schoons were enemies of the state, he felt that as a fighter for *volk en vaderland*, people and fatherland, he had done the right thing.[2]

Some months later while Marius Schoon was away visiting Luanda, the letter bomb was delivered to the Schoon's house. Williamson believed that as nothing had been heard for so long, something must have gone wrong and the bomb had not been delivered. He was wrong. The letter bomb was finally delivered on 28 June 1984. Accompanied by her six-year-old daughter Katryn, the unsuspecting Jeanette took the letter into the kitchen while her three-year-old son Fritz was in the process of toddling off to the landing. Jeanette opened the letter and the bomb detonated. The force of the explosion decapitated Jeanette, tearing off an arm and a leg. Blood sprayed the walls of the kitchen. All that remained of Katryn was a small pile of human flesh. Three-year-old Fritz was left with the gruesome remains of his mother and sister.[3]

On 17 September 2004, after the Slovo daughters and the Schoon family had taken the amnesty ruling by the Truth and Reconciliation Hearings on review in an attempt to overturn that ruling, Craig Williamson signed a deal with the two groups to pay R100,000 toward legal costs and R325,000 to the families to be paid at the rate of R50,000 per month over six months with a final payment of R25,000 (exchange rates were now around R11 to £1). He agreed that if he defaulted on the payments interest would accrue on the outstanding amount at the rate of 15.5 percent per annum. Williamson reneged. In August 2005 the high court ordered that Williamson pay the outstanding amount plus interest. No money was forthcoming. In August 2006 the court ordered the sheriff to attach his property. When the sheriff caught up with Williamson on 22 January 2007 Williamson pleaded poverty and claimed that he was unable to make the payments. Nor was the sherriff able to attach any assets. Williamson's luxury home in the exclusive Beaulieu Estate in Kyalami, and his 4x4 with personalized number plate CMW001 were registered in someone else's name. According to newspaper reports at the time, he was the registered owner of four businesses, his name consistently mentioned in relation to diamond mining in Angola. Undeterred, in November 2007, the twenty-six-year-old son of Marius and Jeanette Schoon moved to sequestrate Williamson. Fritz Schoon argued in his affidavit that Williamson was evading the payment of his indebtedness by either failing to disclose or concealing property and assets that he owned. On 27 May 2008 the judge ordered the sequestration of Williamson's estate.[4]

Williamson today is the owner of the only cigarette-manufacturing company in Botswana, Benson Craig (Pty) Ltd.

# 6. ASSASSINATING TWO HEADS OF STATE

Olof Palme, Sweden's prime minister, was not afraid of ruffling Western feathers, particularly those of the U.S. He was a friend of Cuba's Fidel Castro, the U.S.'s enemy number one; he supported the Palestine Liberation Organization; he criticized American involvement in Vietnam and he openly and actively supported the ANC and the liberation struggle against the apartheid government.

By 15 October 1985, based on earlier intelligence reports, South African Military Intelligence had drawn up a top-secret report that was submitted to the State Security Council outlining the funding provided by Sweden to the ANC—to the extent of 890 million krona (approximately R600 million or £50 million)—and the dangers of Sweden's anti-apartheid stance. The report concluded that Olof Palme was a major threat to South Africa and "must now be considered an enemy of the state". The most damning paragraph concluded the report: "Action proposed against Mr Palme should now be given urgent attention." Someone from the SSC had handwritten in black ink next to that passage: "Agreed!"

An operation, codenamed Slingervel (slingshot), was approved by the SSC with Williamson and Longreach being informed. Final written confirmation was provided by a letter drawn up in General Neels van Tonder's name but signed on his behalf by Tolletjie Botha:

> This is to confirm the verbal briefing that approval for the relevant operation has been received from the highest level. Approval has been granted for the operation to coincide with the planned anti-apartheid assembly in Stockholm in 1986.
>
> It will be ... under the direct command of CSI: Operations.
>
> Suitable personnel will be seconded to Operation Longreach ... Final planning will be handled by Brussels.
>
> The hardware will be provided by the regional representative National Intelligence in Bonn.
>
> The designated operator will commence intensive training immediately and a similar training weapon will be provided by NI head office.
>
> The operator will be deployed in the operational area at the last possible moment to ensure maximum personal security. The correct name of the operation is 'Slingervel'.
>
> This confirms that the primary target of the operation is the subject 'OP'.

TOP SECRET

15 OCTOBER 1985

MILITARY INTELLIGENCE REPORT

SUBJECT: ANTI SOUTH AFRICAN ACTIONS: SWEDEN.

1. Further to previous Intelligence Reports circulated, (MI Reports dated 17 January 1985, 9 April 1985, 19 September 1985) the following have to be brought to the State Security Council's notice:

1.1. It has been confirmed that Anti Apartheid Movements would be congregrating in Stockholm, Sweden during February 1986 for a conference.

1.2. The ANC, has historically obtained about 50% of their finacial support from Sweden and has had the support of Mr. Olaf Palme, the Premier of Sweden, who is at the forefront of European Action against South Africa. (Please refer to MI Reports of 17 January 1985 and 16 July 1985 detailing Mr. Palme's anti South Africa actions).

2. Reliable Swedish Sources confirmed that Mr. Palme's sympathies towards the U.S.S.R. have caused grave concern in Sweden and that these sympathies would most certainly have a detrimental effect on the influence of the U.S.S.R. in Europe and Africa.

2.1. Mr. Palme can be seen as a major contributor against South Africa and should now be seen as an Enemy of the State.

2.2. The previously suggested action against Mr. Palme should now receive urgent attention.

3. The Anti Apartheid Conference in Stockholm, it is suggested by our Swedish Sources in Uppsala, would present the ideal opportunity to take the necessary action against Mr. Palme and it would be possible to ensure that the action be attributed to other groups.

4. It is therefore suggested to the SSC Working Committee that the necessary approval should now be obtained without delay.

TOP SECRET

Military Intelligence report on Olof Palme. (South African History archives / De Wet Potgieter collection)

0128

3

THIS IS A FREE TRANSLATION FROM "AFIKAANS" TO "ENGLISH" OF A DOCUMENT THAT IS DATED ~~04~~ 22 NOVEMBER 1985 THAT WAS CLASSIFIED AS "TOP SECRET"

TRANSLATION:

TOP SECRET

MEMORANDUM TO:

THE MANAGING DIRECTOR
LONG REACH

GUIDE LINES FOR THE EXECUTION OF OPERATION "SLINGERVEL"

This is to confirm the verbal briefing that the approval for the aforementioned operation was received from the highest level.

The operation has been approved to co-inside with the planned anti-apartheid rally in Stockholm in 1986

It will be a combined Special Intelligence Operation but it will resort directly under the command of CSMI Ops.

Suitable personnel will be attached to Long Reach for the duration of the operation.

The surveillance operation that will be needed, will be under the control of Brussels, with the cooperation of Paris, Bonn and the "Uppsala Group"

The final planning and co-ordination will be under the control of Brussels.

The Regional Representative of NI in Bonn will supply the hardware.

The Operator to be attached will be made available immediately for intensive training and a similar weapon for training will be made available from NI HQ. The Operator will be deployed in the operational area, at the last moment to ensure maximum personal security.

TOP SECRET

Translation of top-secret document outlining plans for Longreach and Olof Palme. (South African History archives / De Wet Potgieter collection)

(No 1. ?)

(6)

THIS IS A FREE TRANSLATION FROM "AFIKAANS" TO "ENGLISH" OF A DOCUMENT THAT IS DATED 22 NOVEMBER 1985 AND IT IS THE SECOND PAGE OF A DOCUMENT TAT WAS CLASSIFIED AS "TOP SECRET"

TRANSLATION:

TOP SECRET

Page 2

The correct operational code name is "Slingervel" (note this means "sling-shot" – translators note)

It is confirmed that the primary target for the operation would be "OP"

All communication regarding the operation will be handled by MI (translators note Military Intelligence) and will be classified as "Top Secret" through out. It is therefore important that firm/strict security should be maintained through out without exception.

A further order-group would be held during the next week and a warning- order will be signalled within 48hours.

Note that all personnel concerned must be present at the next order-group.

..........................................

Maj. Gen. N. van Tonder (Signed by T (?) Botha Colonel – Translators note)
C.S.M.I. Ops

(Chief Staff Military Intelligence Operations – Translators note)

Olof Palme in the early 1970s. (Oiving)

5

NOTES ON THE SECOND PAGE OF THE DOCUMENT.

THERE ARE A NUMBER OF MARGIN NOTES SCRIBBLED IN AFRIKAANS AND A FREE TRANSLATION OF THESE ARE AS FOLLOW:

NOTE 1: The English needs no translation. The "RA" is clearly initials. The initials could most likely refer To the operator selected and could be "Roy Allen"

NOTE 2: "Make Sure" or "Ensure" This most likely refer to the Security aspect of the operation that seems to have been a worry to the writer.

NOTE 3: "Please inform Williamson of how it is done"

This refers to how a Military Order-group is conducted in a strict formal manner. Williamson it is assumed to be the same person as Craig Williamson who was never trained as a Military Officer and would not have acted as one which would have annoyed any Senior Military Personnel present.

It is clear that the person who ever made the notes on the file copy was aware of this and requested that Williamson should be taught how such an order-group is conducted.

It cannot be confirmed but it would seem as if the writer was either general van Tonder himself or Vice Admiral Dries Putter, who would have been over-seeing such an important operation.

Place of Olof Palme's murder: taken from the southwest corner of the crossing of Sveavägen, Tunnelgatan and Olof Palmes gata. The exact place of the murder is where the three girls, to the right of the Kreatima sign, are standing. The killer ran into Tunnelgatan (between Kreatima and the T-sign). The shop was called Dekorima in 1986. (Tage Olsin)

Next to the final paragraph someone had scrawled, "Inform Williamson how it is to be done please."[1]

From 21 February through to the 23rd a massive anti-apartheid rally was held in Stockholm, Apart from more than a thousand delegates from the world's anti-apartheid movements, including the Swedish People's Parliament Against Apartheid, leaders of the ANC in exile such as Thabo Mbeki and Oliver Tambo were in attendance. Included in the large crowds at the rally were South African undercover agents. Oliver Tambo addressed the crowd but Palme's speech was the one that inflamed emotions. He deviated from his notes and lashed out at the South African government for its policy of apartheid and called for the release of Nelson Mandela. However, no incident took place.

Investigative journalist De Wet Potgieter writes in his book *Total Onslaught* that the assassin flew into London on the morning of 24 February and stayed that night and the next in the Grosvenor Hotel, Hyde Park. He took a ferry to Amsterdam on the morning of 26 February whence he travelled to Denmark where he checked into a guesthouse. On the 27th he travelled to Sweden and stayed at the Hotel Wellington in Stockholm. He probably made contact with the Slingervel advance team and radical right-wing Swedes for an operational planning session. The decision was taken to go ahead with Slingervel the next night, 28 February.

On that fateful night, Olof Palme had given his bodyguards the night off as he had decided to take his wife Lisbet to the cinema. On a bitterly cold but clear night, Palme and his wife were walking out of the cinema in Sveavagen, discussing the movie they had just seen. A man walked up to the couple and at very close range fired two shots. Palme was hit in the back and fell to the ground. The second shot seared Lisbet Palme's back without penetrating the skin. She hardly noticed the burning sensation as she bent over her fatally wounded husband. A cab driver summoned the police on his cab radio. The fifty-nine year-old Palme was rushed by ambulance to hospital but was declared dead on arrival.

The assassin probably left the country immediately. He spent the next night at a guesthouse in Amsterdam and then took the ferry back to England. He stayed at the Yacht Hostel in London on the night of 2 March and flew back to Johannesburg on the night of 3 March. Two weeks later he submitted his expense claims to Longreach for his overseas expenses. They were authorized on Craig Williamson's behalf by Riaan Stander.

The weapon used was a .357 magnum revolver. Police found no bullets at the scene of the shooting. However, a bullet was picked up by a women at the scene of the shooting on 1 March, supposedly the bullet that had wounded Lisbet; another bullet was picked up at the scene on 2 March, supposedly one of the bullets that had fatally wounded Palme. No bullets were found by the police at the scene immediately after the shooting so it would appear likely that the bullets found four days after the shooting had been planted to cause confusion.[2]

S E C R E T

DMI. INTERNAL AUDITOR
Date: 22/07/86
DIR. DIV. FIN

INTERNAL MEMORANDUM

DATE: 14 March 1986
TO: CRAIG WILLIAMSON MANAGING DIRECTOR, LONGREACH
FROM: ROY ALLEN
REGARDING: OPERATION "SLINGERVEL" (SLINGSHOT) - RECONCCILIATION EXPENSES AND PERSONAL CLAIM

---

I have had the following expenses during the participation of the abovementioned operation and herewith ask for the approval of the following:

UNITED KINGDOM:
Hotel Expenses: 24 February to 25 February 1986

| | |
|---|---|
| Grosvenor Court Hotel, Hyde Park | US $ 213,50 |
| Travel Expenses (Taxi and Under Ground) | US $ 25,00 |
| Telephone Expenses (Public) | US $ 70,00 |
| Meals | US $ 86,75 |
| Ferry Expenses to Amsterdam, Holland | US $ 35,00 |

DENMARK:
Hotel Expenses: 26 February 1986

| | |
|---|---|
| Guest House | US $ 150,00 |
| Car Hire and Fuel | US $ 345,00 |

SWEDEN:
Hotel Expenses: 27 February 1986

| | |
|---|---|
| Hotel Wellington | US $ 80,00 |

HOLLAND:
Hotel Expenses: 29 February 1986

| | |
|---|---|
| Guest House, Amsterdam | US $ 50,00 |
| Ferry Expenses to United Kingdom | US $ 35,00 |

GOEDGEKEUR/APPROVED
Datum/Date..1986-03-1?
Stander
P.P BD./MD
LONGREACH

S E C R E T

Roy Allen's expense claim approved by Williamson. (South African History archives / De Wet Potgieter collection)

S E C R E T

DMI. INTERNAL AUDITOR
Date: 22/07/86
DIR.DIV.FIN

UNITED KINGDOM:

Hotel Expenses: 30 February 1986

| | |
|---|---|
| Yacht Hostel, London | US $ 30,00 |
| Under Ground to Airport | US $ 10,00 |
| Airport Meal | US $ 15,00 |
| | US $1 145,25 |

Cash Slips Attached.

CAPT ROY ALLEN

The same names as those frequently mentioned in connection with the Smit murders keep cropping up: Phil Freeman, Roy Allen, Dries Verwey and the link, Craig Williamson.[3] In 2016 it was announced that the Swedish government had appointed Chief Prosecutor Krister Petersson, effective February 2017, to reopen investigations into the death of Olof Palme. No South African had applied for amnesty in connection with Palme's assassination. Of course, if amnesty had been applied for and granted, it would only have been applicable in South Africa: the perpetrator could still be tried and convicted in Sweden. Williamson denies any knowledge of Palme's assassination despite a sworn statement from Eugene de Kock to the TRC that Williamson was involved.[4] Chief Prosecutor Petersson confirmed that investigations were ongoing and that Swedish investigators had visited South Africa to explore the South African connection. A report by the Swedish authorities confirms that Williamson's involvement is frequently mooted.

The second head of state to be eliminated in 1986 was Samora Machel, president of Mozambique. Speculation is still rife that despite the findings of the Margo Commission which investigated the crash of the Russian-made Tupolov TU 134A-3 that killed Machel and twenty-four others on 19 October 1986 and which concluded that the cause of the crash was pilot error, the shadowy figures of the CCB and the security services still loom large.

The aircraft was returning from Zambia after a Lusaka summit when it crashed into the mountains near Mbuzini, not far from Komatipoort. The site of the crash is located in a small triangle where the borders of South Africa, Mozambique and Swaziland meet. The findings of the Margo Commission concluded pilot error; however, much evidence points at the involvement of the security services in placing a decoy beacon which caused the aircraft to deviate from its course to Maputo into the mountains.

In 1974, weary of conflict in Africa, Portugal, after a left-wing coup, agreed to the transfer of power to Frelimo, the primary liberation movement in Mozambique. Frelimo, backed by the communists, created a new problem for South Africa: on her doorstep the Soviet proxy neighbour was supplying material support and sanctuary to the ANC. Secret meetings were held between South Africa and Mozambique, on 5 May and 20 December 1983, initiated by Pik Botha, South Africa's minister of foreign affairs.[5] These talks resulted in the signing of the Nkomati Accord, a non-aggression treaty between the two countries. Both countries undertook to refrain from interference in the affairs of the other, with neither country allowing its territory to be used as a base for acts of aggression against the other. Despite the agreement, attacks across the border into South Africa continued. At the same time, South Africa was providing covert aid to RENAMO (Mozambican National Resistance) in the civil war with Frelimo.

Samora Machel on a state visit to East Germany in 1983, here seen meeting Premier Honecker's wife, Margot, at a function in East Berlin. (Hubert Link / German Federal Archives)

Relationships between the two countries deteriorated rapidly. On 6 October 1986 six South African soldiers were injured in a landmine explosion close to the Mozambican border. General Magnus Malan warned the Mozambican government that in the ten months of 1986 to date twenty-three ANC terrorist attacks had taken place on South African soil. He warned Mozambique that it was "going to clash head on with South Africa".

An urgent meeting of the Frontline States was called on 12 October to discuss the activities of RENAMO troops supported by South Africa and her ally Malawi against Frelimo in Mozambique.[6] On 19 October Samora Machel, before leaving for a meeting with the Zambian president Kenneth Kaunda, briefed journalists, party leaders and military commanders, informing them that he had received information that the South African government intended killing him.

That same day, 19 October 1986, the Tupolev TU 134A-3 aircraft C9-CAA captained by the Russian pilot Yuri Novodran who had twenty-five years' flying experience, with a Russian crew flew President Machel to Mbala in Zambia for discussions with President Kaunda on the deteriorating situation with South Africa. After the meeting the aircraft took off from Mbala at 1638 bound for Maputo. No flight plan was logged. The estimated time of arrival in Maputo was 1925. At 1902 the aircraft began its descent toward Maputo. The heading of the aircraft changed from its mean of 189° to 184°. Maputo control advised the aircraft to report again at 3,000 feet. From an altitude of 5,200 feet, with Maputo ahead and slightly to the left, with the South African–Mozambican border on the right, the aircraft descended to 3,000 feet.

The aircraft was low on fuel and flying on autopilot. At 1910 when the aircraft was a hundred kilometres from Maputo,[7] the navigator started turning 37° to starboard.

"Can't it be straight?" asked Novodran.

"VOR [Very High Frequency Omni Directional Range] indicates that way," was the navigator's reply.[8]

The aircraft was now heading toward the mountains of the escarpment and not toward Maputo as the crew believed. At 1918 the aircraft reached 3,000 feet and notified Maputo that they were maintaining that altitude yet, despite that, they continued to descend. No warning was given from the South African air traffic controller at the SAAF airbase at Hoedspruit who was monitoring the flight.

Seven minutes before their estimated time of arrival the crew peered into the dark, searching for the runway lights or the lights of Maputo.

"There is no Maputo," Novadran announced. He assumed that there was a power failure in Maputo. "Electrical power is off, chaps!"

The aircraft continued its descent. The crew became disorientated. Still believing that they were descending toward the runway, even when the ground-proximity warning system sounded for thirty-two seconds, they continued their descent. Seven seconds after the alarm stopped, at 1921, the aircraft struck the ground at a height of 2,187 feet.[9] President Machel and twenty-four others were killed on impact.

A Zambian pilot, Frankeson Zgambo, had been recruited and trained by Craig Williamson to gather information on Samora Machel. This was acknowledged by Williamson but claiming he knew nothing of a plot to assassinate Machel.[10] An SAAF flight sergeant told the commission of inquiry that he had seen a friend building a decoy beacon at 4AD Snake Valley (Swartkop airbase) near Pretoria, in 1986. He provided drawings and technical details. He confirmed that the beacon disappeared off the base over the weekend of the crash and was returned after the crash.[11] There were allegations that Cornelio Vasco Cumbe (alias Roberto Santos Macuacua) who worked at the control tower at Maputo airport had been recruited by South African security police and that he had switched off the Maputo VOR at the time the rogue VOR was switched on.[12] Both Maputo and Matsapha (Swaziland) airport companies were run by a known member of the Italian Mafia with strong ties to the South African security police. Both VORs would have had to have been nullified to allow the rogue signal to be received.[13]

There was a strong military presence in the area of Komatipoort and Mbuzini the night of the crash. A former MI officer testified that he had been based at Skwamans, a secret security police base near Komatipoort, and that a number of high-ranking security force officials had attended a meeting and a *braai* at Skwamans the day before the crash. Some returned after the crash. The names he provided in a sworn statement included Foreign Minister Pik Botha, General Kat Liebenberg, General van der Westhuizen of Military Intelligence, as well as Captain Wayne Lelly who headed up a secret base, Sub-station 4, which overlooked the mountain where the plane crashed. According to the MI officer, some of the operatives went to the sub-station at the crack of dawn on the day of the crash. Skwamans was closed down shortly after the crash.[14] When I asked Pik Botha whether he had been there he responded, "That is a blasphemous lie."

Neil Barnard head of the National Intelligence Service admitted that documents were removed from the scene of the crash for copying.[15] General Lothar Neethling refused to hand over the cockpit voice recorder (black box) and delayed the investigation into the crash for several weeks.[16] The track of the aircraft at the time of impact was on a line which would have taken them to the north of the Matshapa beacon, which, as claimed by the Margo Commission, was the beacon that the crew had accidentally switched onto. They were therefore *not* being guided by the Matshapa beacon, but rather a rogue beacon placed by South African security police.

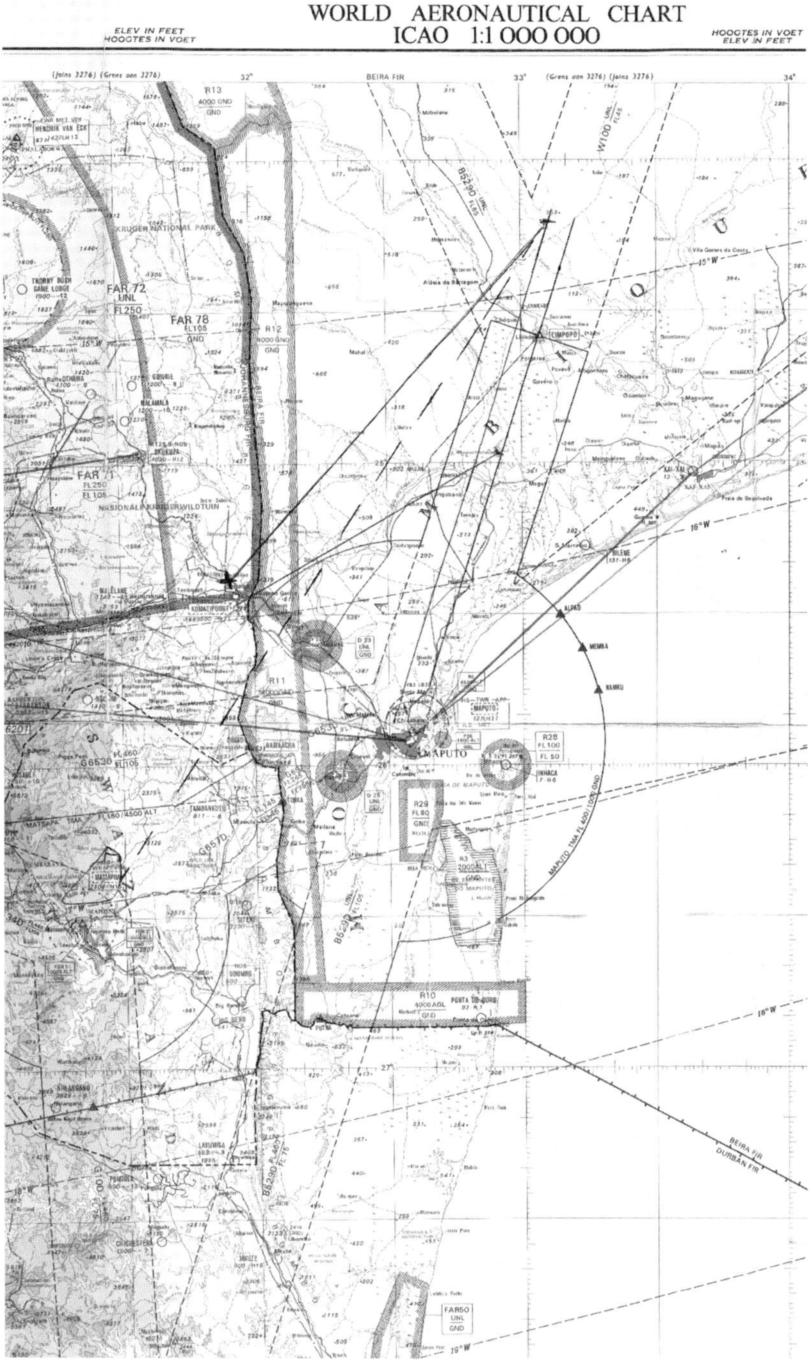


The author's flightpath calculations. Machel's aircraft followed the bold vector upper outer left. (Robin Binckes)

# 7. ON THE PRESIDENT'S ORDERS

Frequently the operatives from Vlakplaas worked with regional offices of the security police on particularly sensitive or complex operations. Sometimes, if the enemy didn't exist, they created their own. One such incident became known as the DairyBelle murders where Vlakplaas operatives assisted the Western Cape Security Police under Major-General Griebenouw, firstly to create an enemy and then to eliminate it.

In late 1985 'Mr Fix It', Eugene de Kock, was approached by Griebenouw to assist in an operation in the Western Cape against 'terrorists' believed to be operating from the DairyBelle Hostel in the Gugulethu township. The hostel was home to thousands of male workers who worked for the DairyBelle ice-cream company. De Kock appointed Riaan Bellinghan to head the operation and briefed the Vlakplaas team that included Bellinghan, Joe Coetzer, Johannes Liebenberg, Thapelo Mbelo, and other askaris like Gladstone Mose, Eric 'Shakes' Maluleke and Jimmy Mbane.

The team travelled down to the Cape by minibus and based up at the police camp at Koeberg. At their briefing seven men were identified to them as being involved in planning an attack on the police. Unsuccessful attempts were made to infiltrate Mbelo into the confidence of the residents of the DairyBelle Hostel to ascertain who the terrorists were. However, two other askaris, Mbane and Maluleke, succeeded in penetrating the circle. Over a period of time they managed to convince a number of people that they were ANC activists. In January 1986, the Vlakplaas team drove into Cape Town with three vehicles. One carried weapons and explosives concealed inside. Mbane and Maluleke then drove to the house of Yamile, a well-known community leader, and told him that they were MK commanders. When they showed Yamile the contents of the minibus he was convinced of the authenticity of their story and introduced the two men to 'Piet', one of the seven ANC activists and supposed leader. Piet fell for the story to the extent that Mbane and Maluleke even assisted Piet in fixing his faulty AK-47. It soon became apparent that Piet was the only one of the seven to have undergone military training and the only one with a weapon. Undeterred, the Vlakplaas operatives set about equipping them all to become terrorists. For the next two months Mbane secretly carried out combat training for the seven, while Maluleke instructed them with political indoctrination.

Eventually, an attack that would target a police bus transporting senior policemen to Gugulethu station was planned for 3 March 1986. This information was conveyed by Mbane to Bellinghan and Liebenberg who prepared for the event.

On 3 March 1986, twenty-five heavily armed police were briefed and deployed from Wingfield naval base at 0300. By 0500, the intended target area was surrounded. Mbane, driving a stolen bakery van, dropped the seven youths off at the site around 0725. Allegedly, grenades were thrown by the Gugulethu Seven and the police opened fire from all sides. Reports say that Piet was the only one who had time to return fire. When the shooting began one of the askaris, Mbelo, saw one of the seven, 'Rastaman', fall as he was hit by bullets. Mbelo stopped his vehicle as another of the seven ran up and offered to show Mbelo where others were hiding. A white sergeant came up to Mbelo and ordered him to shoot the man standing in front of them with his arms raised in surrender. Mbelo obliged and shot the man in the head. The police sergeant then said, "*Man, jy skiet kak*" (Man, you shoot shit) and shot the man again as he lay on the ground, this time in the stomach.

All seven of the Gugulethu Seven were killed by shots to the head. One of them had his face blown away. Piet was shot twelve times in the head. The men were Mandla Simon Mxinwa, Zanisile Zenith Mjobo, Zabonke John Konile, Themba Mlifi, Godfrey Jabulani Miya, Christopher Piet and Zola Alfred Swelani. For their help in exposing and leading the Gugulethu Seven into the ambush, Mbane and Maluleke were each given R7,000, a thousand for each of the seven.

The murder of ten young activists three months later was a direct result of a death squad initiated by the Northern Transvaal Security Police. As the liberation struggle escalated, more and more young ANC activists were becoming involved in the insurgency with many secretly undergoing military training in Botswana. Special Forces were aware of this and the main exfiltration route through Zeerust in the Northern Transvaal into Botswana was identified. The term 'instant training' was used to describe the training which was held over weekends. Recruits would be driven to Botswana on a Friday, receive a module of training over the weekend and be back at work, if employed, on Monday morning in Johannesburg with no one any the wiser. A recruit might make the weekend journey a number of times until his training was complete.

Charl Naudé, a CCB operative, met with Brigadier Jack Cronjé in June 1986 to discuss future operations. Cronjé expressed concern about the streams of recruits travelling to Botswana for military training. It was decided to target the next group being transported for these purposes. Naudé was informed by Cronjé that the security police had been able to infiltrate the ANC and therefore had advance information as to who next was likely to be sent for training and when.

Naudé and Cronjé then began planning. Naudé reported back to General Joubert and outlined their plan that included the administration of drugs to their victims. As the required drugs had a scheduling status, they needed the general to authorize procurement. Naudé ordered his medical rep, Dave Tippet, to procure the drugs from a physician. When this had been done, Naudé, and Cronjé met Rudi Craus of the security police in Zeerust and drove to a secluded spot some distance from town where they planned to carry out the operation.

That evening they set up the ambush. Major Derek Vorster was placed in a lookout position on the track approaching the ambush site to warn Cronjé and Naudé should any outside person accidentally approach. Cronjé and Naudé then waited for the arrival of the VW Kombi (minibus) carrying the ten unsuspecting recruits driven by the infiltrator, Joe Mamasela, the former Vlakplaas askari who had fallen out with de Kock and now worked for the Northern Transvaal security branch, to arrive. An hour and a half after the appointed time they heard the Kombi approaching. The three men, each carrying a weapon, crouched and waited. As the Kombi came to a halt at the chosen spot, Naudé grabbed the handle of the Kombi door and slid it open. There were startled shouts from the occupants but no avenue of escape as three rifles were covering the only exit

One by one the men were ordered out of the vehicle. Tippet filled the syringes while Naudé injected the ten men. Immediately the victims clambered back into the Kombi where they very quickly lost consciousness. The whole process took less than fifteen minutes. By the time the last man was injected the first five were already unconscious. Cronjé and Naudé peered into the dark interior of the Kombi and could make out the slumped shapes.

Naudé slammed the door closed and said, "Let's go!"

Colonel Craus then led off in another vehicle as Vorster climbed into the driver's seat of the Kombi carrying the victims and followed Craus's minibus with Commandant Naudé and Brigadier Cronjé aboard. After driving for some forty-five minutes, Vorster's two-way radio crackled: "This is the place," came the voice of Naudé.

Vorster stopped his vehicle and climbed out, leaving the engine running and headlights on. He looked around. The headlights cast an eerie light over the dirt track and he could see that they had stopped in a dry riverbed. The lead vehicle's tail lights glowed an angry red through the blackness of the night, having stopped a hundred metres or so on the other side of the riverbed. Thirty metres and dead ahead of the Kombi and in the full glare of the headlights stood a tall syringa tree. Perfect, thought Vorster. He climbed back into the vehicle, fastened his safety belt, gunned the accelerator and aimed the Kombi straight at the tree. There was a loud crunch as the Kombi, travelling at about 40kph, rammed into the tree, then dead silence broken only by the *tick tick* of metal cooling. The ten occupants were still unconscious. Vorster then climbed out of the vehicle, retrieved a twenty-five-litre jerry can of petrol from the back, slid open the door and poured the contents over the unconscious recruits. He then tossed in a burning match. There was a *whoosh* as the Kombi burst into flames. As he walked to Craus's minibus up ahead, guided by the red lights, one of the men from the Craus's vehicle passed Vorster in the direction of the burning Kombi. He tossed a limpet mine into the funeral pyre together with an AK-47 to create the impression that the vehicle was carrying ten terrorists and had skidded off the road into the riverbed, where it had crashed into the tree and exploded on impact. There was a massive explosion as the limpet mine detonated. Later at the Truth and Reconciliation hearings it was heard that several of the victims were under sixteen.[1]

Dr Fabian and Florence Ribeiro. (*In the Heart of the Whore* by Jacques Pauw, published by Southern Book Publishers)

Dr Fabian Ribeiro and his wife Florence ran a medical practice in Mamelodi township north of Pretoria. They were ANC activists and many of their patients were wounded ANC operatives on the run from the police. Their activities had not escaped notice. A file on them had already been opened containing details of their operations as well as aerial shots of their house. There were claims by the security police that the Ribeiros were training young activists to become terrorists. The file was ready for the day when the order came to eliminate them.

In late 1986, the commander of the Northern Transvaal security branch, Charl Naudé, briefed Noel Robey on the contents of the Ribeiros' file and informed him that he was eliminate the Ribeiros, and that two hitmen from northern South West Africa (Namibia) had been flown in to carry out the murders. He instructed Robey that he was to familiarize the two assassins with the area of Ribeiros' house and assist them in carrying out the assassination.

Robey collected the two on their arrival in Pretoria. They introduced themselves as John or Gao Pinta and Louis da Silva. Robey introduced himself as Lionel Kirby (most CCB and the security police operatives used false names). Sitting in his car behind the Special Forces HQ, Robey briefed the men on the Ribeiros and the location. After showing them two hotels, the Victoria and the Manhattan, he told them to choose one where they would spend the night. He then dropped them off at the Pretoria station, instructing them to meet him there at eight o'clock the next morning.

At 0800 the following morning Robey drove up in a blue Golf and found the two men standing where he had dropped them off the night before. Painstakingly, he showed them the route out along Church Street to Mamelodi and the Ribeiros' house and where they were to rendezvous once the 'hit' had been made. Robey made the two men rehearse the route six times during the course of the day to ensure there would be no slip-ups. In the meantime a red Opel sedan had been left at the Palm Hotel in Pretoria for the pair to use to carry out the assassination.

On the third day Robey again met the two at the station and drove with them to the Ribeiros' house and clinic, two separate buildings some distance apart. The three men spent the day reconnoitring the premises until Robey was satisfied that the two hitmen were completely familiar with the buildings and layout.

That evening he phoned Charl Naudé: "Everything is fine, there will be no hiccups. The two know the route and everything is fine from our side."

"I'll come back to you," said Naudé.

The next day at about eleven thirty in the morning, Robey received a call from Naudé. "Carry on with the operation. But you must wait until this afternoon, after four o clock, because that's when Ribeiro and his wife get home from their surgery."

Robey then collected from Die Gat two Colt .45s fitted with silencers as the standard police-issue 9mm pistols were traceable back to the security forces. He stashed the pistols in a duffel bag stuffed with towels.

He then phoned the two assassins. "Meet me at the usual spot at half past three. It's on."

Driving his personal Land Rover, he picked up a colleague, Vlietstra, who was to accompany him. On this fateful day, after picking up Vlietstra, he drove to the station, parking some distance off as he did not want the assassins to see Vlietstra. He walked across and handed the duffel bag to da Silva. "It's on. You know the way. Go and do it." He watched as the men drove off in the red Opel.

Robey and Vlietstra then drove the Land Rover to the Schoemann Street carpark to pick up the blue Golf where Robey always parked it. There they would leave the Land Rover. When Robey attempted to start the Golf the engine refused to fire. After fifteen minutes, it became apparent that the battery was dead. Sweating and flustered the two men then drove to the Palm Hotel in Robey's Land Rover where Naudé was waiting for them. When Robey explained what had happened with the Golf, they discussed aborting the operation, but it was too late: the assassins were on their way. Naudé instructed Robey to carry on and to use his own vehicle, the Land Rover, to meet the killers at the rendezvous.

Da Silva and Pinta had meanwhile arrived outside the Ribeiros' house. They could see that the Ribeiros had already returned after their day at the surgery. They knocked on the door. It was opened by Dr Ribeiro. The two men shoved them into a courtyard. When Dr Ribeiro and Florence saw the Colt .45s they both began to scream. The killers opened fire, hitting Ribeiro with a number of shots in the chest. Blood spurted and Ribeiro fell dying on the floor. Florence Ribeiro had been standing behind her husband.

She screamed as the assassins fired again, pumping several bullets into her. She fell, dying in a pool of blood. Da Silva and Pinta ran for the car. The whole operation had taken only a few minutes but already, drawn by the screams, a small crowd of neighbours had gathered outside. When they saw the two men running from the house there were shouts of, "There they are. Get them!" Da Silva and Pinta fired a few shots in the air and the crowd scattered. The two men jumped into the red Opel and with tyres squealing roared away. The two drove to the rendezvous point where Robey was waiting next to the Land Rover as he realized that the assassins would be looking for the delinquent blue Golf. Vlietstra then jumped into the red Opel and drove off to dispose of the weapons while the two assassins climbed into the Land Rover with Robey and returned to Pretoria. At five o'clock the next morning Robey collected the two men and drove them to Special Forces HQ whence they flew back to South West Africa never to be seen again.[2]

As the Eastern Cape security police developed a reputation as an efficient killing machine, the Northern Transvaal branch came to be viewed in much the same way and was particularly active in eliminating perceived enemies of the state. Two of its most notorious killers were Warrant Officer Paul van Heerden, known as 'The Electrician', and the other, one of the most callous killers in the security police, Joe Mamasela. Mamasela had been a student at the time of the Soweto uprising of 1976. He went into exile and joined MK. After being captured and tortured, Mamasela 'turned' and became an askari serving at Vlakplaas where he became one of their most effective killers. After a row with the commander Eugene de Kock, who Mamesela thought planned to kill him, he was transferred to the Northern Transvaal security branch where he joined van Heerden and Captain Jacques Hechter

Joe Mamasela. (*Dances With Devils* by Jacques Pauw, published by Zebra Press, an imprint of Struik Publishers)

One of their most infamous killings was that of Harold Sefola and his two colleagues, Jackson Maake and Andrew Makupe. In 1986 Sampina Bokaba, a Northern Transvaal security policeman, together with Warrant Officer van Wyk, recruited Jackson Maake to infiltrate ANC networks in Botswana. Bokaba was Maake's handler together with Hechter and van Vuuren. When Maake returned from a trip to Botswana, Hechter suspected that he had become a double agent. Maake was picked up by van Vuuren and Mamasela and taken to a deserted property owned by the Portland Cement Company some five kilometres outside Messina near the Zimbabwean border. After van Vuuren had applied a series of electric shocks to him, Maake confessed that he was working for the ANC and named Andrew Makupe as his MK contact.

The next day Makupe was picked up by Mamasela and van Vuuren and taken to a deserted mine property where he was interrogated. Under duress Makupe broke and told van Vuuren and Mamasela that Harold Sefola was the MK operative who selected their targets and who acted as their ANC courier. Van Vuuren took Makupe to a telephone box and instructed him to call Sefola to tell him to expect to be collected by some ANC comrades that night in Witbank in the Eastern Transvaal. Later that night Mamasela and van Vuuren picked up the unsuspecting Sefola. His interrogation began the next morning. At one stage Mamasela forced a sharp knife up Sefola's nostrils. After this Sefola spoke more freely. Still suspecting that he was withholding information and determined to squeeze every drop of information from him, van Vuuren hooked up the electrodes to Maake, cranked up the generator and electrocuted him in front of Sefola. He was about to do the same to Makupe when Sefola asked van Vuuren if he could say something. Van Vuuren agreed.

"May I sing *Nkosi Sikelel'i iAfrika* [*Gold Bless Africa*] before you kill me? One day the ANC will govern and democracy will be the end for the Boers."

President P. W. Botha ordered the bombing of COSATU House.

Mamasela had an ANC flag that he draped over Maake's body while Makupe and Sefola sang. As their voices faded, van Vuuren upped the power of the generator and electrocuted Makupe before doing the same to Sefola. The three bodies were loaded into a minibus and somewhere in Bophuthatswana, a black 'homeland' in the Western Transvaal, the minibus was blown up by a landmine to create the impression that the MK soldiers had died due to their own incompetence.[3] The killings of Maake, Makupe and Sefola are immortalized by Judith Mason and her triptyque of paintings titled 'The Blue Dress' that today hangs in the Constitutional Court of South Africa

In March 1987 Brigadier Willem Schoon again briefed de Kock and this time ordered him to bomb COSATU House in Johannesburg. He informed de Kock that the order had come from President P. W. Botha.

Judith Mason's 'The Blue Dress'. (Robin Binckes)

De Kock purchased torches, rope, bolt cutters and arranged AK-47 rifles fitted with silencers to be made available to the team selected to carry out the bombing. From the rooftop of a building across the road from COSATU House his men kept a watch on the comings and goings. In addition de Kock sent one of his men into the building with a camera concealed inside his briefcase to film the interior. The explosives were prepared in conjunction with the SAP's explosives unit. Explosives of Soviet origin were selected to give the impression that the explosives had been stored inside the building and had accidentally detonated. More than fifty kilograms were used which was, in de Kock's opinion, enough to wreck the building.

Two months after the briefing they were ready. On the night of 7 May the bombing party set off from a safe house in Honeydew on the outskirts of Johannesburg after removing anything that could identify them as policemen in case things went wrong. They doctored a few cans of beer with drugs in case they needed to incapacitate any guards on site. Accompanied by Brigadier Schoon, the Vlakplaas men arrived at COSATU House soon after midnight. The bars to the basement windows were cut and the explosives specialist climbed down a rope to set the two charges, one of twenty kilograms and the other of thirty. It took him less than five minutes. After the explosives had been placed the team drove to the East Rand and waited. They did not have long to wait. There was a massive roar as the explosives detonated and the night sky lit up with the flash of the blast. There were high fives all round as COSATU House was demolished.

In August 1988, on the instruction—this time of General Gerrit Erasmus, who again confirmed to de Kock that the order had come directly from P. W. Botha—to blow up Khotso House, the building which housed the headquarters of the South African Council of Churches, de Kock met with Captain Charles Zeelie who was attached to John Vorster Square, SAP HQ in downtown Johannesburg. It was believed that ANC operatives were using the building as a safe house where they could plan terrorist attacks against state targets. Zeelie informed de Kock that he had been assigned the task but admitted that he had failed. De Kock was amused to learn that Zeelie had been transporting several Soviet TM-57 landmines in plastic Checkers bags—Checkers is a major supermarket chain—to carry out the bombings but the bags had split with the wayward landmines rolling down a central Johannesburg pavement.

Again a meeting was held at the safe house in Honeydew. De Kock asked General Erasmus what he should do if challenged by ordinary members of the SAP not involved in the plan. Erasmus replied, "Shoot them."

On the night of 31 August the men left the Honeydew house in three vehicles. A VW Kombi carried the 'penetration' team and a Nissan Laurel and a Ford Sierra carried the 'stop-gap' teams who were to keep watch while the penetration team did its work. The two stop-gap vehicles parked between Khotso House and the railway station. Their job was to keep watch and prevent any interference by regular members of the SAP or anyone else for that matter.

The penetration team gained access to the basement and de Kock, who had reduced the amount of explosives to be used to between sixty and eighty kilograms, placed the explosives next to a pillar near the lifts and set the detonators. While they were busy setting the explosives a patrolling policeman peered down from the road toward the basement but saw nothing to arouse his suspicions. The three cars then left the scene and drove into Hillbrow to await the explosion. When it came the blast shook Johannesburg and the building collapsed. Nineteen people were injured in the blast. The teams then returned to Honeydew to a celebratory *braai*. A few days later at a function at Vlakplaas attended by high-ranking police officials Minister of Police Adrian Vlok made a speech congratulating the Vlakplaas team on their success. A few months later Vlok, wishing to create a smokescreen, publicly lied and fingered Shirley Gunn, an ANC activist, as the bomber. She was arrested with her sixteen-month-old son and detained for sixty-two days before being released without charge.[4]

Based in Paris from 1983, Dulcie September was the ANC's chief representative for France, Switzerland and Luxembourg. She had been recruited into the ANC after becoming active in the anti-apartheid movement in London after she had left South Africa having been detained without trial for her political activities. She was an outspoken advocate of arms sanctions and the military isolation of South Africa and called on the French government on a number of occasions to impose total economic and military sanctions against South Africa. She was actively investigating clandestine arms deals between South Africa and France despite the official stance of the French government in supporting sanctions. She faced increasing harassment from the France political hierarchy who were sympathetic to the apartheid government and attracted the attention of the French intelligence services. Her handwritten notes published by the *Daily Maverick* 20 September 2017 include notes with regard to arms and oil deliveries to South Africa. She refers to a shipment of arms on a ship called the *Tinemaru* which had been used extensively to ship arms to the apartheid government by a Danish shipper Jorgen Jensen.[5] Because of her activities and vocal demands she was aware of being under surveillance. In 1985 she wrote a report to the ANC and detailed some of the threats: her offices and home phones had been bugged, she had seen people on more than one occasion taking photographs of her at a station and her office had been broken into more than once. Late at night she would receive mysterious phone calls. She specifically mentioned a journalist, Jean-Paul Horeau, who had been pestering her for an interview to discuss the ANC's relationship with the French government.[6] For her troubles, however, she developed a reputation in the corridors of the ANC for being an alarmist.

Dulcie September Square in Paris. (Pierre-Yves Lambert)

On the morning of Tuesday, 29 March 1988, as Dulcie September, holding her unopened post in her one hand, opened the door of the ANC office at 28, rue des Petites-Ecuries, Paris, with her other, five shots from a .22-calibre pistol fired at point-blank range struck her in the face, killing her instantly.

Eugene de Kock informed the TRC that a French mercenary, Jean-Paul Guerrier, was involved with her murder[7] under the direction of Dawid Fourie, deputy head of the CCB[8] while Jacques Pauw mentions Dirk Stoffberg who headed up the CCB Z Squad in Europe and who paid two French legionnaires £20,000 each for the murder.[9] Craig Williamson denies any involvement in the killing of September but admits that "she was a target". The TRC found evidence that the security police were involved in her killing.[10]

# 8. APARTHEID CRUMBLES

From the time of his fall from favour, the disgraced former commander of Vlakplaas, Dirk Coetzee, nursed a grudge against his former colleagues and felt that he had been unfairly treated. At any opportunity, and particularly after a few drinks, he would tell whoever was listening of his role in the death squads. Few, with one exception, paid attention. In 1984 Coetzee had befriended Frans Whelpton who at the time was in partnership in a business venture with Brigadier Jan Blaauw. Both men were under investigation for extortion and corruption. Coetzee tipped the men off that the police were tapping their phones and that a 'sting' operation using illicit diamonds as bait was being planned against them. As a result Coetzee himself now became the target of police spying and harassment. He began to drink heavily. Whenever possible he told whoever would listen of the illegal police phone-tapping as well as the activities at Vlakplaas. Most people dismissed his rantings as those of a drunkard but the one man who listened was Jacques Pauw. Pauw, at the time, was an investigative journalist with *Rapport*, a Sunday Afrikaans newspaper. Sensing the opportunity of a big story, Jacques cultivated a friendship with Coetzee over a period of time. Pauw also spoke to his direct superior at *Rapport*, Max du Preez, and told him of the Vlakplaas stories that he had heard from Coetzee. The two knew that there was little they could do with the information at the time, as the editor of *Rapport* was Wimpie de Klerk, the brother of Minister of Internal Affairs F. W. de Klerk.

Accompanied by his friend Whelpton, Coetzee went to see Wynand Malan, the National Party MP for Randburg (now part of Greater Johannesburg) and told him about his activities at Vlakplaas. There was no reaction. He then paid a visit to Koos van der Merwe, a member of the right-wing Conservative party. Van der Merwe gave his report to the head of the party, Dr Andries Treurnicht, but again nothing happened. Coetzee's world was collapsing around him. After a police investigation and seven charges against him, Coetzee became embroiled in a defamation case brought against him by two of his police colleagues. Coetzee believed that there was a conspiracy against him in the police and that there had been attempts to kill him. After exaggerating the seriousness of the diabetes that he suffered, Coetzee was declared medically unfit and was discharged from the South African Police on 31 January 1986.[1]

Throughout this time Jacques Pauw frequently met Coetzee but, fearing reprisals, Coetzee refused to tell all. He also believed that if he told Pauw the whole story he would be implicated in murder and charged. Matters came to a head in 1989. By this

Almond Nofomela (left) and Dirk Coetzee at the TRC hearings. (*Apartheid's Friends* by James Sanders, published by John Murray Press, an imprint of Hodder & Stoughton)

time Pauw and Max du Preez had left the employ of *Rapport* and were running the left-wing Afrikaans weekly *Vrye Weekblad* (*Free Weekly*).

The lid popped when Almond Nofomela, one of the askaris involved with Coetzee in the murder of Griffiths Mxenge, was charged with the murder of a white farmer. The murder was unrelated to any Vlakplaas activities and Nofamela was found guilty and sentenced to death.

He was held in Pretoria Central on death row awaiting execution. Unperturbed by his impending fate, as a member of the Vlakplaas death squads he believed that the police generals would orchestrate his release. As the date of his execution, 20 October, drew closer, Nofomela began to sweat. He sent a message to the new commander of Vlakplaas, Eugene de Kock, urging de Kock to assist in staying his execution. The message he received back was simple and clear: "Take the pain."

Nofomela was desperate. Also on death row were four men known as the Balfour Four who had been sentenced to death for carrying out a sabotage attack on the Sasol (the oil-from-coal processing plant) installation at Witbank. Nofomela, desperate to stop his execution told the four that he was a member of Vlakplaas, home of the death squads. This information was given by the four to their lawyer, twenty-four-year-old Bheki Malangeni who worked for a prominent human rights lawyer Peter Harris of the firm Cheadle Thompson & Haysom. Harris couldn't believe his good fortune. The media had for some time speculated on the existence of death squads and for

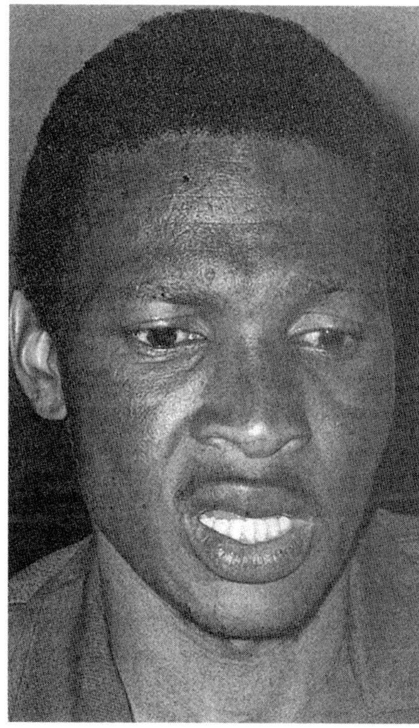

Almond Nofomela who chose not to "take the pain". (*Apartheid's Friends* by James Sanders, published by John Murray Press, an imprint of Hodder & Stoughton)

months Harris and others had been attempting to gather evidence that the government operated death squads. This had now fallen into his lap. Harris obtained an urgent court injunction and Nofomela was granted a stay of execution.

The story of Nofamela's stay of execution made the newspapers and Coetzee knew that either he would now have to spill the beans and by doing so position himself as the hero or that the full story would be released by others and he would become the villain. Still nervous, he tentatively agreed to talk to Jacques Pauw but realized that his life would be in danger once he spoke. He asked Pauw to arrange protection for himself from the police who he believed would kill him once it became known that he had gone public with his exposé. Pauw spoke to Max du Preez and the two decided that the only way they could publish the story would be if Coetzee was out of the country and had protection.

Quick to try to put a lid on the whole affair Minister of Justice Kobie Coetzee appointed a commission of inquiry to investigate Nofomela's claims. Pauw and du Preez knew the furor that publishing Coetzee's story would cause. They also saw the story as being a major boost to their struggling newspaper *Vrye Weekblad*, so long as the story could be verified. There was only one route Pauw could go to get protection for Coetzee: through the ANC in exile. Through his contacts Pauw approached André Zaaiman, a regional director of the Institute for a Democratic Alternative for South Africa (IDASA) who Pauw knew had direct contact with the ANC in exile. After clandestine meetings with Pauw, Zaaiman and Coetzee the ANC agreed to grant protection to Coetzee outside South Africa. The jumpy Coetzee insisted he be accompanied by David Tshikalanga, one of his fellow askaris. To ensure Coetzee's protection, Pauw decided that it would be better if he and Coetzee flew to Mauritius, interview Coetzee there and send the tapes back to South Africa for publication in *Vrye Weekblad*. Tshikalanga was to make his own way to meet the ANC in Zimbabwe. At the last minute Coetzee got cold feet and refused to leave. After hours of persuasion he finally agreed to go. Both Pauw and Coetzee feared for their lives if news broke of what they were planning.

Pauw collected Coetzee at 0600 on the morning of 5 November 1989 and they set off from Pretoria to Jan Smuts airport, Johannesburg. Both men were nervous and when Pauw's car ran out of petrol still some ten kilometres from the airport, they were in such a flap that they decided to abandon the car and thumbed a lift from a passing vehicle rather than delay by trying to find petrol and possibly missing their flight. The two were terrified and sweating profusely when they finally passed through passport control without incident. Every second they expected a member of the security police to apprehend them. On board the aircraft, before it had taken off for Mauritius, Coetzee ordered a bottle of Moët & Chandon. Safely in Mauritius, over the following few days Coetzee told Jacques Pauw in detail of his activities at Vlakplaas and the involvement of his superiors in the South African Police. On Friday, 17 November, under the headlines "Bloody Trail of the SAP", *Vrye Weekblad* broke the story. It was picked up internationally and made headlines around the world: "South Africa Runs Death Squads".

Vlakplaas had also become one of the best-equipped armouries in the country. In the late 1980s de Kock had instructions from Brigadier Willem Schoon to procure

The corpse of a SWAPO guerrilla strapped to the mudguard of a Koevoet APC. Koevoet operators were paid a bounty for each guerrilla killed or captured. (Attie Hattingh via Leon Beizuidenhout)

SWAPO guerrillas in Ovamboland. (Leon Bezuidenhout collection).

captured communist weapons from Ovamboland in northern South West Africa from the SADF and Koevoet bases at Oshivelo and Ondangwa. Many of the operatives at Vlakplaas, including de Kock, had been members of Koevoet, the much-feared and respected police unit. Whenever the weapons stockpile in Ovamboland grew big enough, General Hans Dreyer would tell Schoon to come and collect.

'Fok-Fok'.

De Kock himself went on two trips to Ovamboland and sent other operatives on at least two other occasions. According to de Kock (as told to Jeremy Gordin) in *A Long Night's Damage*, de Kock stated that on one of the occasions he also brought two Unimog vehicles and trailers back to Vlakplaas for Brigadier Schoon who claimed them as his personal property but instructed de Kock to say that they were for the use of Vlakplaas. More than sixty tonnes of arms and ammunition were brought to Vlakplaas, including SAM-7s, AK-47s, RPD machine guns, grenades, explosives, limpet mines, mortars, RPG rocket launchers and ammunition of all sorts,[2] as well as a fair sprinkling of SADF weapons such as R1 and R4 rifles. The weapons were stored at Vlakplaas to be used by Vlakplaas death squads as well as regional security services, in counterinsurgency operations, in assassinations and for planting 'evidence'.

After the exposure of the existence of Vlakplaas and the breaking of the story worldwide, Vlakplaas was thrust into the media spotlight resulting in a frenzy of activity on the farm. Eugene de Kock was furious at Coetzee's betrayal and swore revenge. He and his men acted swiftly to hide any evidence of the true purpose of

'Team-building' for Vlakplaas operatives and friends, on the Natal South Coast. (*Dances With Devils* by Jacques Pauw, published by Zebra Press, an imprint of Struik Publishers)

Vlakplaas from the eyes of the media. He was warned by General Stadler to get rid of anything that might stoke the suspicions of visiting media. Thirty steel cases were used to conceal weapons and ammunition and were taken to the nearby police farm Daisy. At the time there were more weapons held at Vlakplaas than at any large military base in South Africa. Soon afterward de Kock was forced to remove the weapons store again when Daisy later cropped up in the Harms Commission. This time arms and ammunition were transported to the Police College in Pretoria and the balance to the government-owned arms manufacturer, Mechem, also in Pretoria, for storage.

During the 1980s de Kock frequently supplied other police units and on at least one occasion the SADF who used the communist-manufactured weapons to create a fictitious ANC arms cache that enabled the army to claim an excuse for a cross-border raid into Botswana.[3]

After the media frenzy, to complete the air of normality all documents at Vlakplaas were burned in a 210-litre drum and askaris were sent undercover to Swaziland to hide.[4] Journalists who visited the farm were told that it was a South African Police training base and were introduced to a few selected 'tame' askaris who vehemently denied the existence of anything other than a normal police base. In an attempt to swiftly put a lid on the stories of Vlakplaas and the CCB, the government appointed Justice Louis Harms to establish a commission of inquiry into the existence of death squads. The earlier commission had soon been recognized as a police cover-up.

Orders were then given to de Kock to kill Coetzee, who by this time was in Zambia en route to London and safety. De Kock had become obsessed with killing Coetzee. He obtained a video of Coetzee talking to a journalist and showed it to key members of Vlakplaas, instructing them to "watch carefully". Because one of the operatives, Sergeant Bellinghan, known as 'Balletjies' (Small Balls), had been a friend of Coetzee's, de Kock tasked him with deciding on the best way to kill Coetzee. Bellinghan suggested a bomb. He remembered that both he and Coetzee were great fans of the singer Neil Diamond and that gave him the idea of how to ensure Coetzee's death. De Kock instructed Captain Kobus Kok to make two bombs and so the ordnance department of the South African Police began the task of building the bombs. In the meantime Sergeant Steve Bosch was instructed to purchase a pig's head and bring it to Vlakplaas.

When the bombs were ready they were brought to Vlakplaas. In a test watched excitedly by Vlakplaas operatives and askaris on the banks of the Hennops river, de Kock switched on the cassette player triggering the bomb. The pig's head disintegrated into fragments of flesh and bone splinters. Satisfied that the bomb would work, the other bomb was then packed into another cassette player, a Sony Walkman.

Two tapes were included. One was titled 'Evidence of Hit Squads', the other 'Songs by Neil Diamond'. Either, it was felt, would be sufficient to whet Coetzee's appetite to insert one of the tapes into the Walkman, switch it on and blow himself to smithereens. The parcel was assembled in the room at Vlakplaas that was used as an armoury and addressed to Coetzee at P. O. Box 34077, Lusaka, a postbox provided to him by the ANC. On the reverse side of the parcel they wrote the name and address of the 'sender': Bheki Malangeni, Cheadle Thompson & Haysman. Carefully wrapped in untraceable material by Kobus Kok and Bellinghan who were both wearing gloves as they worked, the package was then taken to a Pretoria post office and dispatched.

Coetzee and his ANC-appointed 'minder' who had been appointed by the ANC head of intelligence, Jacob Zuma, in response to Jacques Pauw's request for protection for Coetzee, were notified in November 1989 of the arrival of the parcel at the Lusaka post office. Coetzee was immediately suspicious. Accompanied by his minder Stanley, Coetzee called in at the post office on their way to Lusaka airport where he was to join Pauw before the two flew to London to give evidence in a defamation case. When Coetzee was handed the parcel he became agitated and immediately claimed that it was a bomb. He refused to take the parcel and noticed the name of the 'sender' on the back of the parcel, Bheki Malangeni. He turned to Stanley: "I'm not taking this parcel. It's a bomb. I'm damn sure it's a bomb. They have put the name of Bheki Malangeni as the sender on the parcel ... he's going to get it sent back to him. You must get a message to Malangeni and warn him."

Stanley nodded.

At the airport the highly strung Coetzee was more agitated than normal when he met Pauw: "They have sent me a parcel, Jacques. They are trying to kill me. It's a bomb, I'm certain."

Pauw was sceptical: "I don't think they would try that."

"Of course they would. They're after me. You must warn Bheki Malangeni that he is going to get the bomb because they have put his name on the back as the sender of the parcel." Irritated by Pauw's skepticism, he turned to Stanley: "You must warn Malengeni, Stanley, you must warn him."

Both men forgot.

After three months in the Zambian and South African postal systems, the tattered parcel was placed in Bheki Malangeni's pigeonhole in the Cheadle Thompson & Haysom post room on 12 February 1990 (the day after Nelson Mandela's release). There it remained for three days before being collected by Malangeni on 15 February. He was on study leave for his attorney's admission exam. The night before, being Valentine's Day, he and his wife had celebrated with a family dinner and had cut their wedding cake, which they had not cut on the day of their wedding. Malangeni tore off the wrapping in the post room and placed the small cardboard box taped with transparent tape in his briefcase. That night he and his wife went to the movies at the Kine Centre on Commissioner Street in downtown Johannesburg. They watched *Reversal of Fortune*.

When they got back home to the suburb of Jabulani, Soweto, Bheki told his wife that Dirk Coetzee had sent him a parcel and that he was going to listen to the tape. He went to the section of the bedroom that served as a study and sat at his desk and opened the parcel. He could see the Neil Diamond tape in the machine through the transparent cover of the Walkman. He pushed the eject button. The tape slid out and he popped 'Evidence of Hit Squads' in. He put on the earphones that had been included in the parcel, sat back in the chair and pushed the play button. The room and Bheki Malangeni exploded in a ball of fire.[5]

Over the next few years Coetzee was to move thirty-eight times for fear of elimination by the Vlakplaas death squads. With the publicity surrounding Coetzee's exposé of Vlakplaas and its operations tensions ran high on the farm.

Brian Ngqulunga, one of the askaris who had played a role in the murder of Griffiths Mxenge, feared that his part in the killing would be exposed and that he would face murder charges. He began to panic. At Vlakplaas word spread that Ngqulunga wished to give evidence to the Harms Commission and that he had switched allegiances to the ANC. General Nick van Rensburg instructed de Kock to eliminate him. When Brian

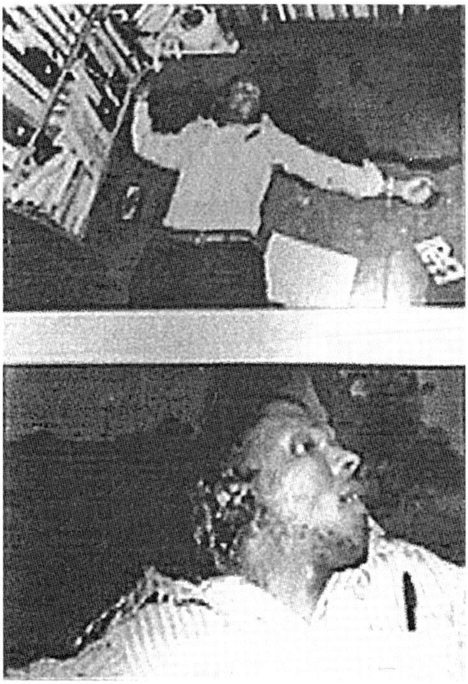

A very grainy photograph of Bheki Malangeni, blown up by the Walkman bomb. (*Dances With Devils* by Jacques Pauw, published by Zebra Press, an imprint of Struik Publishers)

Ngqulunga, suffering a nervous breakdown, shot and wounded his pregnant wife three times de Kock instructed one of his men, Dave Baker, to arrange his killing. A hit squad was assembled which included Wouter Menz, Piet Botha, Willie Nortje and Riaan Bellinghan. They hired a VW Kombi and lured Ngqulunga away from the police office where he was now working. When he drove into their trap the Vlakplaas operatives, faces covered with balaclavas, dragged Ngqulunga from his car, bound him, taped his mouth and assaulted him before dumping him bloodied and whimpering into the Kombi where they continued to assault him. In terror Ngqulunga urinated in the Kombi. They then dove to a deserted road near the town of Brits, north of Pretoria. Here they pulled a terrified Ngqulunga from the vehicle and, as he lay on the ground, Bellinghan emptied an AK-47 magazine into Ngulunga's head, shooting away part of his face and his tongue. A stream of yellow bile shot from Wouter Menz's mouth as he vomited at the sight of his former colleague's face shot away. Botha then emptied his service pistol into the corpse. They left the body on the side of the road for the police to find, hoping that they would think that it was an ANC execution.

The hit squad then drove to a farm north of Pretoria where they hosed down the inside of the vehicle to clean away any trace of Ngqulunga's blood and urine. They then met with de Kock to celebrate the success of the operation by having a few drinks and a meal at the Holiday Inn. When the regular police contacted de Kock and informed him that they had found the body of one of his men, de Kock ordered that he be given an official police funeral at Vlakplaas. The men who had killed him stood at the side of the grave on a hill overlooking Vlakplaas. All the men involved were at his funeral, except Menz, who remained in the canteen. When questioned later by de Kock as to why he had not been at the funeral, Mentz replied, "I don't think it's right to kill a man and then be one of the mourners at his funeral."[6]

Nine months after the establishment of the Harms Commission to investigate the existence of death squads in South Africa, Judge Harms concluded: "There is no evidence of death squads in South Africa."

After the breaking news of the existence of the death squads in *Vrye Weekblad* in 1989 and the intense media interest that followed, the operations of Badger Unit (Vlakplaas) were scaled down and the role of Vlakpaas changed. It was given the task of fighting organized crime in Hillbrow, a notoriously sleazy part of Johannesburg governed by gangsters, drug peddlers and illicit diamond-dealers. Their 'administration' flourished. The CCB was already operating in Hillbrow and thus CCB and Vlakplaas joined forces. Ironically, the offices of the CCB were for a period located at The Fort, now the home of the protectors of democracy, the Constitutional Court. Weapons were stored in cells in the women's gaol.

One of the most notorious gangsters in Hillbrow was Alex Kouvaris, a convicted drug-dealer who had been recruited into the ranks of the CCB as an 'unaware' operative.

The women's cells in The Fort where CCB operatives stored their weapons. (Robin Binckes)

In 1989 CCB operative Staal Burger flew with Kavouris to London to set up an import-export company. According to evidence led at the Truth and Reconciliation hearings an amount of R70,000 (£16,500) was provided by the CCB for this exercise. The money went missing: it was suspected that Kouvaris and Burger had divvied up the money for themselves.

At the same time, Eugene de Kock issued instructions that four Vlakplaas askaris—Ndam, Sebole, Stretcher and Vietnam—who were known to be HIV-positive were to be sent into Hillbrow with the explicit purpose of visiting two brothels located in the Chelsea Hotel and Little Rose Hotel to have sex with prostitutes who would in turn pass on the AIDS virus to the prostitutes' clients, many of whom had been identified as 'the enemy'.[7]

With all the publicity surrounding the exposure of Vlakplaas, a wave of paranoia swept over the regional security police branches, particularly the Eastern Cape. Nic van Rensburg received information that four black policemen who had participated in the killings of the Cradock Four in 1985 were considering 'spilling the beans' about their involvement in the murders. Again Eugene de Kock was called in from Vlakplaas to assist in the elimination of Glen Mgoduka, Amos Faku, Desmond Mapipi and Sheperd Shakati.[8] Major Vaal du Toit who was the technical unit commander at Vlakplaas, assisted by Jacobus Kok, built a bomb which was fitted into a car by Snor Vermeulen and Lionel Snyman. On 14 December 1989 Major Gerhardus Lotz drove the bombed-up car to Port Elizabeth, where it was issued to the four black policemen. The bomb was detonated by remote control, killing all four.

From the mid-1980s South Africa was a country under siege. Violence rocked the townships around the country and internationally South Africa had become the world's pariah. Economic sanctions were starting to bite, the arms embargo was noose-tight and South African sports teams were banned from international competition. Music and sports boycotts were highly effective and, despite a rash of 'rebel' tours designed to break the sports boycott, South Africa was becoming increasingly isolated.

Against this backdrop President P. W. Botha suffered a stroke. In a bloodlesss coup led by his own cabinet Botha was forced to step down. His more liberal colleague, F. W. de Klerk, after being appointed as acting president, was sworn in as President of the Republic of South Africa in September 1989. By this time the Cold War was winding down with the collapse of international communism, and with it the fear of the *Rooi Gevaar* began to recede. In October 1989, only a month after F. W. de Klerk was sworn in as president, the last bastion of communism, the Berlin Wall, fell. Recognizing that support for the ANC from the communist world was now irrelevant, de Klerk announced on the 2 February 1990 his decision to release Nelson Mandela from prison. Nine days later, as the world watched, Mandela walked out of Victor Verster Prison a free man after 9,377 days. His release was the signal to the country

Right-wing paramilitaries: an AWB rally in Church Square, Pretoria. (Anton Raath)

that change was coming. A vacuum of political power was being created. Instead of the violence diminishing, the fighting, especially in the townships, intensified. The two main protagonists were the ANC, still supported by the SACP and COSATU, and the Inkhata Freedom Party (IFP) which was predominantly Zulu and anti-communist. From the time that Mandela walked out of Victor Verster until the first democratic election of 27 April 1994, more than 14,000 people were killed through political violence, mainly in Natal (and theblack KwaZulu 'homeland') and in the townships on the Rand. Initially it was the ANC and the IFP slugging it out but it was not long before everyone got involved including the extreme right wing, the security police, Vlakplaas and anyone else who wished to carve a future through violence.

While the fighting between the ANC and the IFP raged, on 4 May 1990 the first talks were held between all of the political parties and the government. These talks—CODESA, the Convention for a Democratic South Africa—were to go on for three and a half years as delegates hammered out a road map for the future South Africa. But they did little to assuage the violence.

Despite the air of optimism that began to nervously take hold, that change for the good was coming, the work of the death squads continued unabated. Bheki Malangeni was killed by the bomb four days after Nelson Mandela was released. On 28 April 1990 a letter bomb blew off Father Michael Lapsley's hands, burst his eardrums and blew out an eye. Lapsley had become an anti-apartheid activist after the students' uprising of 1976 and was expelled from South Africa in September that year. He went into exile in Lesotho and joined the African National Congress. Already identified as an enemy of the state by the security police, in a cross-border raid in 1982 the security forces killed forty-two people in an attempt to get at Lapsley who was away at the time. Lapsley moved to Zimbabwe and it was here that the Zimbabwean authorities informed him that he was on a South African hit list and that they would provide him with twenty-four-hour protection. In late 1989 public assurances from the minister of defence, General Magnus Malan, that there would be no further attacks by South African forces on the Frontline States were tentatively welcomed. Then Mandela was released and Lapsley and his minders dropped their guard. Lapsley had recently returned from a three-month-long visit to Canada and was about to start a new job as a parish priest in Bulawayo. While away a large amount of mail had accumulated. One of the letters, on an ANC letterhead and signed by 'Vusi', informed Lapsley that he would be sending under separate cover some religious material that he thought Lapsley would be interested in reading. Lapsley had already collected the package containing the material from the post office, the parcel notification slip having been included in the accumulated mail. He opened the package and inside were two religious magazines wrapped in plastic—one English and one Afrikaans. He put aside the Afrikaans magazine and opened the English one, detonating the bomb.[9]

# 9. FANNING THE FLAMES

While the country's leaders talked and argued about a new political dispensation, the death squad killings continued. In 1992, Sergeant Douglas Holtzhausen, one of the white NCOs at Vlakplaas, approached de Kock and informed him that he had been tipped off by an informant that Winnie Mandela's driver, known as Tiso and a member of the ANC who had received military training, was involved in smuggling arms and ammunition to the ANC and that he was planning an armed robbery in Nelspruit in the Eastern Transvaal to help fund the operation. Holtzhausen told de Kock that he wished to foil the robbery and catch Tiso and his gang. De Kock gave him the go-ahead.

Holtzhausen and Willie Nortje, the two in charge, liaised with de Kock in the planning of the operation. The Vlakplaas team gathered at the Drum Rock Hotel outside Nelspruit and waited for de Kock and Lieutenant Chappies Klopper, who had been attending to other business, to join them. They were delayed. Tired of waiting, as the convoy of vehicles was leaving the Drum Rock, de Kock and Klopper arrived. The convoy set off and de Kock and Klopper followed. When they arrived at the selected ambush site Holtzhausen ordered his men into position to await the arrival of Tiso's minibus that would be indicated by a Vlakplaas BMW that was driving in front of it. The men were equipped with AK-47s and R5 rifles. De Kock positioned himself on a bridge with a view down the road. As he watched, the BMW, driven by Ben Burger van Zyl, approached, leading the targeted minibus. As the BMW neared the ambush site, it accelerated away from the minibus as a hail of bullets raked the minibus, which in turn accelerated before slowing and coming to a halt. De Kock ran from his position on the bridge and fired a large number of rounds into the vehicle. Alarmed at the random and ill-disciplined shooting by the Vlakplaas team and aware that one or more of his own men could be shot by 'friendly fire', de Kock took control and ordered the men to regroup. Much to de Kock's surprise, flames burst from the minibus, followed by a violent explosion that threw one of the occupants into the road where he rolled and rolled trying to extinguish the flames that engulfed him. Apparently a jerry can of petrol and two grenades in the minibus had 'cooked off'.

Van Zyl then informed Holtzhausen that Tiso was not one of the four dead in the minibus. Nortje and Holtzhausen left the scene and sped off in the direction of Nelspruit to find him. They returned shortly with Tiso in tow, having picked him up at the scene of the proposed armed robbery, and bundled him into the boot of Nortje's car. De Kock ordered Rolf Gevers, Charlie Chait and Colonel J. Swart to accompany

Nortje in another vehicle. After travelling on a dirt road for some distance, they were met by two Vlakplaas askaris. Here they transferred the bound Tiso into the Gevers's car. They were instructed to travel with their prisoner to a point where two other Vlakplaas colleagues, Vermeulen and Brits, were waiting for them. Chait and Swart informed Gevers that Tiso would have to be killed as he could identify them as Vlakplaas operatives. Vermeulen and Brits, who were both explosives experts, left Gevers to return to Pretoria to collect some dynamite that they would use to blow up Tiso's body after he had been killed. Later that afternoon, Vermeulen and Brits returned and led the way to a disused mine at Penge.

At the mine Gevers and Brits began interrogating Tiso. When he refused to answer the two men beat him. They alternated beating him with forcing him to take swigs of beer. Eventually, faced with Tiso's silence, they told Tiso that as he had no information, they were going to let him go. They all climbed into their vehicles and headed for an open mine in the complex. Tiso believed that he was going to be released. When they arrived at the open mine Tiso, still with hands tied, climbed out of the vehicle. Gevers shot him three times in the chest and he fell to the ground, dead. Vermeulen,

Askaris at shooting practice at Penge mine. (*Eugene de Kock: Assassin for the State* by Anemari Jansen, published by Tafelberg)

Brits and Gevers then stripped Tiso naked and placed him in a sitting-up position with explosives on his lap. More explosives were strapped to his body. They set the timers and retreated into cover. After a few minutes there was a massive explosion as the dynamite detonated. A large hole marked the spot where the body had been. Worried that all the evidence hadn't been destroyed and as it was getting dark, the men slept in a disused building until dawn when they returned to the hole in the ground. In the early morning light, as they scoured the area, they gathered together bits of body parts and tissue into a pile and blew it up again, repeating the process three times to ensure that nothing remained of Tietsetso 'Tiso' Leballo. The others killed in the attack on the minibus were Oscar Mxolisi Ntshota, Glenack Masilo Mama, Lawrence Jacey Nyalende and Khona Gabele.[1]

On 4 May 1990 the body of Teboho 'Tsietsie' Mashinini, the youth who led the student march on 16 June 1976, arrived back in South Africa from Guinea in a casket. After leading the student march from the Morris Isaacson High School, Mashinini had gone into hiding. He had joined the South African Students' Movement and in the lead-up to the events of 16 June having been elected as chairperson of the Action Committee (later renamed the Soweto Students' Representative Council, or SSRC) which was to challenge the Department of Bantu Education. His allegiance to Steve Biko's Black Consciousness Movement would already have drawn the security police's attention. His knowledge and charisma marked him for leadership, a role that sat easily on his shoulders. In the mayhem that followed the 16 June shootings, despite being in hiding, Mashinini issued a statement condemning the actions of the police: "We see it as an official declaration of war against the black students by our 'peace' officers."[2]

The police failed to track him down, despite offering a R500 reward for information leading to his arrest. They raided his house, only a few hundred metres from the Morris Isaacson High School, on at least two occasions but Mashinini, dressed in woman's clothing, managed to walk out of the house under the noses of the police. Colonel Visser of the Soweto CID appealed through the media for Mashinini to hand himself in, claiming that it was for Mashinini's own safety and protection from angry IFP hostel dwellers, who, Visser claimed were furious at the violence in Soweto. "We believe that Mashinini is active and moving around Soweto and other townships but we have been unable to find him. If you spot him or know where he is you must report him to the nearest police station." Visser attempted to convince Mashinini's parents to persuade him to hand himself in "for his own good".

For two months Mashinini eluded capture but it was obvious that he could no longer lead a normal life in South Africa. In August he slipped over the border into Botswana and joined the thousands of other youth in exile.

His role in leading the march catapulted him to international prominence, particularly in Africa where he was hailed as a hero of the people. After a few months in

Botswana he made his way to West Africa and was received by President Sékou Touré of Guinea. He then lived in Nigeria for a while, addressing the media and giving lectures on the situation in South Africa under apartheid before settling in Liberia where he married a beauty queen and daughter of a parliamentarian. They had two daughters and then divorced. He later visited the United Kingdom and it was on this trip that he, without knowing it, encountered Craig Williamson who at that time was still under cover and working for the IUEF in Geneva.[3] He also visited the United States and addressed the United Nations on apartheid and the situation in South Africa. None of these activities would have endeared him to the security police in South Africa.[4]

The legendary singer and activist Miriam Makeba was a great admirer of Mashinini and offered him a place to stay at her house in Conakry, Guinea. He arrived in Conakry early in 1990 but decided to return to South Africa and participate in the changes that were taking place. Two weeks before returning home Tsietsie Mashinini was savagely attacked and beaten with a blunt instrument. He was taken to hospital but died from his wounds. When his coffin was opened on arrival in Johannesburg friends and family were shocked to see the extent of his injuries. His left eye had fallen out, his face was covered with deep bruises from the beatings, there was a violent gash on his forehead and his left ear had been bleeding.[5] Activist Andile Mngxitama was to say: "I know for a fact that Tsietsi Mashinini was murdered at least two weeks before he was due back in South Africa. I lived with Khotso Seatlholo and other SAYRCO [South African Youth Revolutionary Council] members in Zola [Soweto] and we were preparing for his return—it was a tightly kept secret; he would have gone first to Lesotho to wait things out till Soweto was ready. Tsietsi, like Khotso, was against negotiations, and Soweto was his base. His arrival would have impacted on the political developments in the country." He is buried in Avalon, Soweto, and his grave has been vandalized on at least two separate occasions.

After the release of Mandela, as the battle for power between the ANC and the IFP escalated in the townships and KwaZulu, the better-equipped ANC began to gain the upper hand. It was not long before the IFP turned to the sympathetic anti-communist security forces for clandestine support. It was during this period that Vlakplaas played its most lethal role, fanning the flames of violence and mortgaging the future of the country by pushing it to the brink of civil war.

In 1990 a former Vlakplaas operative Andries 'Brood' van Heerden who worked for ABSA Bank in Johannesburg was introduced to Themba Khoza of the IFP who asked van Heerden whether he could assist with the supply of arms to the IFP. Van Heerden approached Willie Nortje of Vlakplaas and requested his assistance. When Nortje first approached de Kock, de Kock refused, recognizing the dangers of getting drawn into what was tantamount to a civil war.[6]

Both bearded, de Kock (left) and Willie Nortje at a drinks session. Nortje appears to be fingering someone. (*Eugene de Kock: Assassin for the State* by Anemari Jansen, published by Tafelberg)

After a number of requests, de Kock agreed to attend a meeting with two prominent IFP members, Victor Ndlovu and Themba Khoza, at van Heerden's apartment. The IFP representatives asked de Kock to supply weapons to the IFP. Khoza told de Kock that the IFP were poorly trained, had no transport or financial support and that they had to use knobkerries and assegais against the guns of the communist-supported ANC and that because of the lack of means to defend themselves the IFP were being wiped out.[7] Aware that the majority of police and security police supported the IFP rather than the 'communist' ANC, de Kock eventually agreed to assist. "I knew that this assistance was in line with the general feeling about the IFP among police members ... one Captain Frederick Botha, for instance, told me that a massive amount of money was earmarked by the police for the IFP," de Kock later told the TRC in his application for amnesty.[8]

The following evening de Kock again met with Khoza. At the meeting de Kock gave Khoza a shotgun, an R1, ammunition and some Eastern Bloc hand grenades. A few days later Nortje and de Kock loaded weapons into the boot of their car and, accompanied by van Heerden, drove to an industrial area of Johannesburg where they handed the weapons over to Khoza and Ndlovu. This signalled in earnest the commencement of the supply chain.[9]

With Major-General Krappies Engelbrecht and Major-General Nick Janse van Rensburg, the head of Section C, de Kock discussed the IFP request at a function at Vlakplaas. Engelbrecht and van Rensburg gave de Kock the go-ahead and suggested Vlakplaas manufacture firearms for the IFP. Van Rensburg instructed de Kock to submit false expenses claims to the value of the costs of manufacturing. This would amount to R60,000 (£12,000) for a hundred homemade shotguns. They also discussed Khoza's transport problems and de Kock requested permission from van Rensburg to register a 'secret funds' car, a Nissan Sentra, to Khoza. De Kock then contacted two operatives, Snor Vermeulen and Daniel Snyman, to have the designs drawn up.[10] The shotguns were manufactured by Derek Rausch who conveniently had an engineering shop next door to Mechem and who frequently worked for the state-owned arms manufacturer. (Rausch had provided the material and the explosives to build explosive devices which were then supplied out of the Vlakplaas stores.) Working at night, it took two weeks to manufacture the shotguns. Rausch also provided Snyman and Vermeulen with three tonnes of 107mm Chinese rockets and explosives to be used in the manufacture of homemade pipe bombs and hand grenades which the three of them then manufactured at Snyman's house. De Kock, with Jac Buchner, the Natal commissioner of police, then handed over the shotguns to Khoza. An additional 200 shotguns were subsequently manufactured and, on the instructions of de Kock, tested and fired in the presence of General le Roux who declared himself happy with the testings. Homemade shotguns were the tip of the iceberg.

To ensure that there was no evidence of security force involvement in the supply of weapons, Verster, Vermeulen and Snyman had hand grenades, landmines, assault rifles (R1s, R4s, AK-47s etc) and handguns (Makarov and Tokarev pistols) modified by having serial numbers and identity markings removed. Hand grenades were painted black and a piece of gut tied between the lever and the hand grenade to ensure that when it exploded it would be completely destroyed, leaving no evidence of origin. The AK-47s were further modified by removing the butts to make them shorter and thus easier to carry and conceal. Some of the AK-47 barrels were also shortened.

A number of additional meetings were held between Vlakplaas operatives de Kock, Willie Nortje, Chappies Klopper, Piet Botha and Charlie Chait and IFP members Minister C. J. Mthetwa from Natal, Themba Khoza, Humphrey Ndlovu, Ms Dlomo, Victor Ndlovu and James Ndlovu to discuss the supply of arms from Vlakplaas. Nortje delivered the weapons from Vlakplaas to the IFP on a regular basis. De Kock himself also delivered weapons to Reverend Mthetwa's house in Natal on more than one occasion and on another, handed over pistols to him in Johannesburg. The weapons provided were distributed to the IFP hostels, the foot soldiers. In each of the hostels the IFP had appointed an *induna* (chief) who would distribute the weapons to the IFP members. In addition to the hostel-dwellers a number of gangs that supported the IFP were also provided weapons.

As the township fighting between the ANC and the IFP escalated, no fewer than forty-nine massacres occurred on the Reef and in the Vaal Triangle in the two years 1990–92, costing the lives of 1,250 people, an average of twenty-five per massacre.[11]

Many of the killings were as a result of the supply of Vlakplaas arms. De Kock was to say, "The black-on-black violence—Inkhata versus the ANC—that we encouraged was a handy propaganda tool because the outside world could be told with great conviction that the barbaric natives, as might have been expected, started murdering each other at every opportunity. We contributed to this violence for a number of years both passively (by failing to take steps) and actively (by sponsoring training and protecting violent gangs)."[12]

As IFP supporters, armed with guns, hand grenades, explosives, spears and axes were returning from a rally to Sebokeng, a township outside Johannesburg, at about 1 a.m. on 22 July 1990 they randomly began attacking residents. In desperation, SAP assistance—the police station was only 500 metres away—was sought but it took the police four hours to arrive. By the time they arrived the IFP attackers had been cornered by local residents in the hostel. The police then called in the army who arrived in armoured Casspirs and opened fire on the crowd outside the hostel. Twenty-five people were shot dead. Themba Khoza was arrested outside the hostel in the car provided by Vlakplaas with his boot full of the weapons that had been given back to him by IFP hostel residents after the massacre to prevent discovery by the police.[13]

On the night of 12 January 1991 a night vigil was arranged on the eve of the funeral of ANCYL (ANC Youth League) member Chris Namgalembe who had been murdered by gangsters and his body dumped in a rubbish tip. The IFP sent messages

The larger massacres that occurred between 1990 and 1993, part of the so-called 'Reef township war', were:

- Sebokeng massacre on 22 July 1990 (27 killed)
- Tembisa Vusimuzi hostel massacre on 12 September 1990 (25 killed)
- Jeppe Station train attack, Johannesburg, on 13 September 1990 (26 killed)
- Thokoza Hostel attack on 2 December 1990 (30 killed)
- Sebokeng Funeral Vigil attack on 12 January 1991 (13 killed)
- Gobizitwna Beer Hall attack, Sebokeng on 23 May 1991 (13 killed)
- Alexandra Funeral Vigil massacre on 12 May 1992 (15 killed)
- Swanieville squatter settlement massacre, Kagiso, on 12 May 1991 (28 killed)
- Thokoza hostel attack in May 1993 (16 killed)
- Crossroads squatter camp massacre, Katlehong, on 3 April 1992 (21 killed)
- Boipatong massacre, Vaal, on 17 June 1992 (40 killed)[14]

of warning not to stage the funeral in Sebokeng but the family went ahead anyway. A tent had been erected for the vigil while the body of Namgalemba lay in a bedroom in the house nearby. Inside the tent mourners began to assemble for the vigil. They sang hymns and prayed. A few of those in the tent were armed as they had promised the grieving family some form of protection. At about 2 a.m., two groups of men, singing and wearing trench coats, approached the tent pretending to be mourners. Shots rang out. There were screams of terror from inside the tent. The shooting continued for over five minutes as chaos and panic ensued. A hand grenade was thrown into the tent then another. Pandemonium spread as those not yet hit scrambled and dived for cover. Corpses lay on top of friends, family and fellow mourners.[15] When the shooting stopped forty-five people lay dead.

In 1992 Eugene de Kock met Philip Powell at a function. Powell was a senior IFP official and a member of the Natal/KwaZulu provincial legislature. The two men chatted but de Kock was wary of Powell. He approached Colonel Jac Buchner, the KwaZulu police commissioner, who was at the same function and asked whether Powell was somebody "he could walk the road with". Buchner stated that de Kock could trust Powell.[16] The two men exchanged telephone numbers and each went his separate way after the function. A few weeks later Powell telephoned de Kock and the two men arranged to meet at the Centurion Hotel in Pretoria. Powell outlined the difficulties the IFP were still facing in the low-intensity war with the ANC and asked whether de Kock could provide instructors to train IFP members. De Kock agreed that it was something he could assist with.[17] The two met twice more when Powell asked de Kock to provide more weapons and further training.

Soon after de Kock had resigned from the police in 1993 to set up his own arms importing business, he received a phone call from Powell requesting more arms and ammunition. De Kock agreed to assist. He gained access to Mechem where the Vlakplaas weapons were stored by using an old police ID card. Theo van Dyk, the Mechem manager, unaware that de Kock had left the police force, gave permission for de Kock to remove more than sixty tonnes of weapons that were then loaded onto six trucks and driven away by members of the KwaZulu police to Mlaba, the IFP camp in Natal. The weapons included dozens of RPG launchers and rockets, 81mm and 60mm mortar tubes and bombs, hundreds of claymore mines, landmines and grenades, thousands of rifles, shotguns and handguns and an estimated 250,000 rounds of ammunition.[18] Vlakplaas operatives were then dispatched to Mlaba to assist in training IFP members

On 26 April 1994 a raid was carried out by the SAP on Mlaba camp and a large number of weapons were recovered. A further seven tonnes were found in the Nqutu Hills in 1999. To this day a significant quantity of weapons is unaccounted for and KwaZulu-Natal remains a hotbed of armed violence, political and otherwise.

As early as 1988, Wayne Swanepoel, a security policemen, and others initiated the phenomenon of train violence by throwing people off moving trains in an attempt to cause additional friction between the ANC and the IFP. These attacks on trains escalated between 1990 and 1994. In the first attack on a train after 1990, on the Soweto–Johannesburg line, one person was killed and about thirty injured. Between 1990 and 1993, approximately 572 people died in more than 600 incidents of train violence. What started as unplanned group attacks and individual killings became orchestrated incidents involving large groups of people. Gunmen would open fire from station platforms or spray commuters with bullets from inside coaches. Perpetrators of such attacks were intent on causing general terror rather than achieving a clear political objective. The CCB and Vlakplaas were directly responsible for this wave of terror.

Meetings to plan the attacks were held at Vlakplaas. A farm in the Eikenhof area south of Johannesburg was used as a base to house the train killers. Being very dark and speaking very poor English, it was suspected that some of the killers were foreigners. Vlakplaas operatives were kept away from them, so as not to be able to identify them. One of the train gangs from Vlakplaas was comprised of Xola Frank Mbane, Khayo, Sylvester, Mvelase, Shushe, Joss and the commander Kilino. These men would board a train wearing balaclavas. White operatives would paint their exposed skin black. Each operative was armed with an R5 rifle and a 9mm pistol. At a given moment the men would open fire on the occupants of a crowded carriage causing total panic and mayhem. Victims would be pushed from a moving train. Incriminating evidence would be intentionally dropped such as an IFP badge or ANC scarf to provoke retaliation from the other group. These attacks frequently took place on trains carrying one or the other party's mourners to a funeral.[19] According to Wayne Swanepoel, the security police would visit the scene of the massacre afterward to make sure the victims were dead.[20]

On 13 September 1990 two groups of assailants, armed with guns and pangas (machetes), boarded the train at Jeppe station at rush hour. The trains were packed with commuters travelling back to Soweto after a day's work. As the train passed through George Goch station the attackers began to randomly shoot at the passengers, hacking them with pangas in three of the carriages. When the train stopped at the next station, Denver, terrified commuters scrambled down onto the platform fleeing the carnage on the train. But they had literally jumped from the frying pan into the fire: on the platform waiting for them stood another group of balaclava-clad men who opened fire. By the time the shooting stopped five bodies lay on the concrete platform. Fellow passengers covered the corpses with their own jackets in an attempt to dignify the bodies. Books, handbags, shoes, packages and blood pegged out the area. Many of the wounded were carried on the backs of fellow passengers along the railway lines, away from the train. In total the massacre left twenty-six dead and over a hundred wounded.[21]

# EPILOGUE

After the release of the Goldstone Commission report which detailed involvement of the security forces in murder and other atrocities, President F. W. de Klerk established his own inquiry headed by Major-General Pierre Steyn. Steyn submitted his report on his findings to F. W. de Klerk who decided a 'show of force' against the errant senior SADF officers 'named and shamed' in Steyn's report was appropriate. On 19 December 1992, in a purge to stop the violence in what has become known as the 'Night of the Generals', de Klerk fired twenty-three of his most senior officers, including two generals and four brigadiers. Finally, after 27 April 1994, the date of the country's first democratic election, the violence began to subside.

Eugene de Kock took early retirement from the South African Police on 30 April 1993. The cabinet authorized payment of R17.5 million (£3.5 million) to de Kock and eighty-three other Vlaplaas operatives. De Kock was arrested having a quiet drink at Johann Rissik House, an International Police Association guesthouse in Arcadia, Pretoria, on 4 July 1994, after someone had tipped off the police as to his whereabouts. He was taken into custody at the Adrian Vlok police station in Verwoerdburg (now Centurion) and denied bail. He was subsequently transferred to Pretoria Central after a furore when it was discovered that he was being imprisoned in some comfort. Brought against him were 129 charges ranging from fraud to murder. After a trial of almost twenty-one months, he was found guilty of 121 charges, including six for murder, one of kidnapping, one of culpable homicide and many counts of fraud. He was sentenced to two life sentences and 212 years in prison.[1]

Major-General Pierre Steyn. His report led to the 'Night of the Generals' when twenty-three of the SADF's top brass were fired by President F. W.de Klerk.

After the establishment of the Truth and Reconciliation Commission in 1996, de Kock gave extensive evidence of his and others crimes to the commission. Following many rejected applications for parole, De Kock was released from prison on parole in 2015 having served twenty-one years of his sentence. In the latter stages of his imprisonment he worked with the National Prosecuting Authority's Madeleine Fullard identifying graves of missing people, including some of his victims.

After his release from prison, in July 2017, Eugene de Kock checked into a retirement home in Riviera, Pretoria, called 'Ons Tuis' (Our Home). He did not stay long. Two weeks later he had checked out after fifty of the staff had complained to management about his presence. Many refused to serve him. Some complained about his clandestine presence and that unlike the other residents at Ons Tuis, no evaluation of his suitability for the home had been conducted and no history provided. One of the workers reportedly told *The Sowetan*: "We felt our lives were in danger. We were scared. We told them that we don't want to serve him."

De Kock left the retirement home on Wednesday, 19 July 2017 accompanied by six men in a convoy of three cars, destination unknown.[2]

Anemari Jansen, author of *Eugene de Kock: Assassin for the State*, describes de Kock as "a broken man" today. Despite this, rumours persist that he is in contact with many of his ex-colleagues and that we may not have heard the end of him. Today he is protected by the state security services. There exists a strange 'old boys' club' made up of ex-spooks, crooks, victims' relatives, prosecutors, lawyers and associates who make up the inner circle and who keep de Kock's whereabouts secret. The 'good guys'

Ons Tuis, the retirement home in Pretoria that expelled Eugene de Kock after protests from the staff (Robin Binckes)

Eugene de Kock in prison uniform, Kgosi Mampura II Prison, Pretoria. (*Eugene de Kock: Assassin for the State* by Anemari Jansen, published by Tafelberg)

rub shoulders with the 'baddies', swap stories and drink together when they celebrate events such as de Kock's birthday.

In 1989, when Jacques Pauw was putting together *Prime Evil*, a documentary on Eugene de Kock, for the South African Broadcasting Corporation, he contacted de Kock who had begun serving his sentence in C-Max, the maximum security prison in Pretoria (now Kgosi Mampura II Prison). Pauw explained that he was busy with the documentary and that, as he wanted to create a balanced presentation, he was keen to find someone who would be able to make positive comments about him. De Kock immediately suggested his brother but Pauw rejected the idea: "No, I need someone else. Someone who knows you well and would be prepared to comment about you."

"Lucas Kalinos. We served together in Ovamboland, He was and still is my best friend."

"Do you know where he is?" asked Pauw.

"Yes, he's in Shoshanguve [a township north of Pretoria]."

Pauw paused for a few seconds. "I can find him but he probably won't talk to me."

"He will if I tell him it's okay," answered de Kock. "Find him and tell him I want to see him and that he must come and visit me with you."

A few weeks later Pauw returned, accompanied by Lucas Kalinos and his six-year-old son whom Kalinos had insisted be brought to meet de Kock. After the usual formalities the three sat waiting in the visitors' room for the arrival of Eugene de Kock on the other side of the bulletproof glass window. A warder appeared, accompanied by de Kock whose face lit up as he recognized Kalinos. Unable to shake hands the two men held their hands up to the glass as if touching one another. Both were crying. When the men had blown their noses and wiped away the tears, Kalinos said to de Kock, "Eugene, I want you to

Eugene de Kock with one of his best friends and comrade in arms, Lucas Kalinos (left) during training of the first group of Koevoet operators. On de Kock's left is an operator who is known only as 'Jules'. (*Eugene de Kock: Assassin for the State* by Anemari Jansen, published by Tafelberg)

meet my son." He reached for the boy, took him by the hand and gently pulled him to the window. "Eugene, let me introduce you to my son ... Eugene de Kock Kalinos!"[3]

Former minister of police, Adrian Vlok, responsible for many of the orders given to de Kock, runs a charity for vulnerable and homeless black people in a township near Pretoria. In a symbolic show of contrition in 1996, he publicly washed the feet of Frank Chicane, a priest that some years before Vlok had instructed the CCB to kill by rubbing poison into his clothes in his luggage at the airport.

Ferdi Barnard, the CCB killer of David Webster, is serving two life terms and sixty-three years in Kgosi Mampura II Prison. Craig Williamson owns the cigarette-manufacturing company, Benson Craig (Pty) Ltd. in Botswana. Former apartheid-era president P. W. Botha was fined by a court in George in 1989 for refusing to appear at the Truth and Reconciliation hearings. He died on 30 October 2006. F. W. de Klerk, the former resident who released Nelson Mandela and with whom he received the Nobel Peace Prize, heads the F. W. de Klerk Foundation and is part of the international celebrity-speakers' circuit. Jacques Pauw, who exposed Vlakplaas, is the chef in his hotel The Red Tin Roof in Riebeek Kastile in the Western Cape. In 2017 he wrote the all-time South African bestseller, *The President's Keepers*, an exposé of ex-president Jacob Zuma and a book that many believe contributed to the end of Zuma's presidency.

# Notes

## Introduction

1. James Sanders, *Apartheid's Friends: The Rise and Fall of South Africa's Secret Service*, John Murray, 2006, pp. 12-36.

## 1. Apartheid, Wind Of Change And Rooi Gevaar

1. J. K. Cilliers, 'Counter-Insurgency in Rhodesia' in *Terrorism and Insurgency*, Routledge Library Editions, 2016, p. 7.
2. Anthea Jeffery, *People's War: New Light on the Struggle for South Africa*, Jonathan Ball, 2009, p. 41.
3. Maj-Gen B. Mortimer, 'South African Defence Force Involvement in the Internal Security Situation in the Republic of South Africa', submission to Department of Justice.

## 2. Enter Boss

1. Ibid, pp. 150-2
2. Kevin A. O'Brien, *The South African Intelligence Services*, Routledge, 2012.
3. Jacques Pauw, *In the Heart of the Whore: The Story of Apartheid's Death Squads*, Southern Book Publishers, pp.103-4.
4. TRC final report vol. 2, ch. 3, subsection 46: Robert & Jean Smit.
5. Hennie van Vuuren, *Apartheid Guns and Money: A Tale of Profit*, Jacana, 2017, p. 60.
6. Ibid.
7. Ballistics report by Maj Petrus van Schalkwyk, SAHA documents, police file.
8. James Myburgh, *politicsweb*, 7 June 2010.
9. Forensic report, police docket, SAHA.
10. TRC / Smit.
11. *Cape Times*, 22 November 2012.
12. Allister Sparks, *The Sword and the Pen*, Jonathan Ball, 2016, pp. 394-6
13. Sanders, pp. 80-90.

## 3. Vlakplaas And 'Prime Evil'

1. Sparks, pp. 360 70.
2. Pauw, p. 55.
3. Ibid, p. 51
4. TRC final report vol. 2, ch. 3, subsection 47, p. 270, paragraphs 436-43.
5. Jacob Dlamini, *Askari: A Story of Collaboration and Betrayal in the Anti-Apartheid Struggle*, C. Hurst & Co., 2015.
6. Eugene de Kock, as told to Jeremy Gordin, *A Long Night's Damage: Working for the Apartheid State*, Contra Press, 1998, pp. 84-87.
7. Ibid, p. 111.
8. TRC amnesty hearing application: AC/2000/085.
9. Ibid, pp. 122-4
10. TRC amnesty hearing application: AM 5462/97.

## 4. Civil Cooperation Bureau

1. Sanders, p. 326.
2. Ibid, p. 517.
3. Ibid, pp. 327-9

4. Steyn Report, p. 516.
5. Sanders, p. 333
6. TRC final report vol. 2, ch. 2, subsection 38, p. 140, paragraphs 398-418.
7. TRC amnesty hearing application: van der Westhuizen, 9 October 2000.
8. Albie Sachs interview, 27 November 2017.
9. Ibid.
10. Ibid.

## 5. Security Police 'Superspy'

1. De Wet Potgieter, *Total Onslaught*, p. 84.
2. TRC amnesty hearing application: AM 5181/97.
3. Report on Schoon's evidence to TRC, South African Press Association, 4 November 1998.
4. Belinda Beresford, 'The spy who lost it' in *Mail & Guardian*, 29 May 2008.

## 6. Assassinating Two Heads Of State

1. Ibid.
2. Ibid.
3. Ibid.
4. Craig Williamson email.
5. Theresa Papenfus, *Pik Botha and His Times*, Litera Publications, 2016, p. 329.
6. Ibid.
7. Margo Commission, p. 22.
8. Ibid.
9. Ibid.
10. O'Malley papers, ch. 6, pt. 19.
11. Ibid, pt. 34.
12. Ibid, pt. 33
13. Ibid, pt. 32.
14. Ibid, pts 40-44.
15. Ibid, pt. 22.
16. Ibid, pt. 25.

## 7. On The President's Orders

1. TRC amnesty hearing application: AM 7985/97.
2. Ibid AM5470/97
3. TRC final report vol. 2, ch. 2, subsection 38, p. 237, paragraphs 293-305.
4. TRC testimony of Eugene de Kock; De Kock & Gordin; *Mail & Guardian*, 15 December 1994.
5. *Daily Maverick*, 20th September, 2017.
6. Ibid.
7. South African History Online.
8. Maggie Davey lecture.
9. Pauw, p. 208; Davey.
10. TRC final report vol. 2, ch. 2, subsection 39.

## 8. Apartheid Crumbles

1. Pauw, pp. 69-70
2. TRC final report: Provision of weapons to IFP.
3. De Kock & Gordin.
4. Pauw, *Dances with Devils: A Journalist's Search for Truth*, Zebra, 2006.

5. Peter Harris, 'The bomb' in *In a Different Time: The Inside Story of the Delmas Four*, Umuzi, 2008.
6. *Mail & Guardian*, 28 February 1997.
7. TRC special report, episode 68, section 2.
8. Ibid.
9. TRC testimony of Father Michael Lapsley, Day 1, 10 June 1996.

## 9. Fanning The Flames

1. TRC amnesty application hearing: AC/2001/171: de Kock, Brits, Swart, Gevers, Gouws, Klopper, Nortje; Hanekom, Vermeulen, van Zyl.
2. South African History Online.
3. Craig Williamson email.
4. Ibid.
5. Ibid.
6. De Kock & Gordin, p. 234.
7. Ibid.
8. TRC amnesty application hearing: de Kock.
9. Ibid.
10. Ibid
11. TRC final report vol. 3, ch. 6, subsection 75.
12. De Kock & Gordin, p. 100.
13. Ibid.
14. TRC final report vol. 3, ch. 6, subsection 75.
15. 'Massacre of a hero's mourners' in *The Star*, 16 January 2012.
16. TRC final report: Provision of weapons to the IFP.
17. De Kock & Gordin, p. 242.
18. TRC final report: Provision of weapons to the IFP.
19. TRC final report: Allegations of security force involvement in train violence.
20. Ibid.
21. Jeffery, p. 259.

## Epilogue

1. Anemari Jansen, *Eugene de Kock. Assassin for the State*, Tafelberg, 2015.
2. *The Citizen*, 17 July 2017.
3. Pauw discussion.

# Index

## Acknowledgements

My thanks to all who helped me write this book. Firstly, Chris Cocks gave me my first publishing break and continues to support me even from a cold and distant land. Jacques Pauw gave me guidance and direction when I was struggling with structure and, even if it's wrong today, it's a great deal better than it was. Jacques for also introducing me to Vlakplaas. Jonathan Ancer returned my phone calls and provided in-depth information in *Uncovering Craig Williamson* and guidance on certain issues. De Wet Potgieter, author of *Total Onslaught*, took the time to discuss certain points with me. Alan Elsdon, author of *The Tall Assassin: Fiction Based on Facts*, did the same. (I am still trying to sort out the fiction from the facts.) Anemari Jansen, author of *Eugene de Kock: Assassin for the State*, attempted to arrange an interview for me with de Kock but failed through no fault of her own. Eugene de Kock bothered to answer some of the questions I put to him through Anemari but then refused to answer others. Craig Williamson, despite refusing to grant an interview, had the courtesy to answer email questions put to him. Previous members of state security who asked not to be mentioned by name but who were prepared to meet with me and gave me time and information. Former minister of foreign affairs Pik Botha was a most gracious and charming host, even if the most guarded. Former Constitutional Court judge Justice Albie Sachs took the time to talk to me and describe his hell as a victim of the car-bomb attack in Maputo. Dr Torrie Pretorius of the National Prosecuting Authority granted me an interview and discussed with me many of the still unsolved murders but then, after undertaking to assist me with certain information, never replied to my follow-up emails. Krister Petersson of the Swedish Prosecuting Authority had the courtesy to reply to my queries and sent me the report to date on the investigation into the death of Olof Palme. Ken Badenhorst, a vastly experienced airline pilot who many years ago taught me to fly, confirmed my calculations on the flight path taken by Samora Machel's ill-fated aircraft. Eliza Smit gave up her time to meet me and shared her views and information on the murder of her parents. The South African History Archives accessed material contributed by De Wet Potgieter and the police files on the killing of the Smits. Finally, to my wife Margie, thanks as always for your support and encouragement, without which nothing would happen.

**Robin Binckes** was born in 1941 in the Eastern Cape, South Africa. Educated at Umtata in the Transkei, he enjoyed a business career that spanned Public Relations, sports promotion, travel and tourism and food retailing. He has written several historical books on South Africa, including the bestselling *The Great Trek—Escape from British Rule: The Boer Exodus from the Cape Colony, 1836*. He has recently started writing for several Pen & Sword military history series including 'History of Terror'. Inspired by the late David Rattray, he currently works in Johannesburg as a tour guide with his own company, Spear of the Nation, specializing in oratory story-telling.